easy breakfast & brunch

easy breakfast & brunch

simple recipes for morning treats

RYLAND
PETERS
& SMALL

LONDON NEW YORK

Designer Iona Hoyle
Editor Céline Hughes
Picture Research Emily Westlake
Production Gemma Moules
Publishing Director Alison Starling

Indexer Sandra Shotter

First published in the United States
in 2007
by Ryland Peters & Small, Inc.
519 Broadway, 5th Floor
New York, NY 10012
www.rylandpeters.com

10 9 8 7 6

Text © Susannah Blake, Celia Brooks
Brown, Maxine Clark, Linda Collister,
Clare Ferguson, Brian Glover, Clare
Gordon-Smith, Kate Habershon,
Rachael Anne Hill, Jennifer Joyce,
Annie Nichols, Jane Noraika, Louise
Pickford, Ben Reed, Jennie Shapter,
Fran Warde, Lindy Wildsmith, and
Ryland Peters & Small 2007

Design and photographs
© Ryland Peters & Small 2007

Printed in China

ISBN-13: 978 1 84597 485 5
ISBN-10: 1 84597 485 9

Library of Congress Cataloging-in-Publication Data

Easy breakfast & brunch : simple
recipes for morning treats / author,
Susannah Blake ... [et al.].
    p. cm.
  Includes index.
  ISBN 978-1-84597-485-5
  1. Breakfasts. 2. Brunches. I. Blake,
Susannah.
  TX733.E22 2007
  642--dc22

                        2007024124

Notes
• All spoon measurements are level
unless otherwise specified.

• Uncooked or partially cooked eggs
should not be served to the very
young, the very old, those with
compromised immune systems, or
to pregnant women.

• To sterilize preserving jars, wash
them in hot, soapy water and rinse
in boiling water. Place in a large pan,
then cover with hot water. With the
saucepan lid on, bring the water to
a boil and continue boiling for
15 minutes. Turn off the heat, then
leave the jars in the hot water until just
before they are to be filled. Sterilize
the lids for 5 minutes, by boiling,
or according to the manufacturer's
instructions. Jars should be filled and
sealed while they are still hot.

contents

introduction

It is well documented that breakfast is the most important meal of the day but many of us fall into the trap of being in too much of a hurry to eat or drink anything as we fly out of the door to start the day. A look through the tempting range and diversity of recipes in this book could help to change all that.

There are dishes here to satisfy any number of tastes and circumstances. For those who are time-poor first thing in the morning, fruit is the ideal way to go, whether in the form of a nutritious smoothie or a scrumptious compote enlivening a bowl of homemade granola. Baked goods are a winner any time. Many of the recipes keep for several days and freeze well, so even if you are on the run, you can take them along as a packed breakfast.

Weekends, vacations, sleep-overs and house-parties provide the perfect excuse for blurring the boundaries between breakfast and lunch. The socializing opportunities a breakfast or brunch get-together offers are second-to-none: the atmosphere is decidedly relaxed and informal, and its timing allows everyone to head off to different activities satiated and energized, and still with much of the day free.

Wherever possible, use fresh seasonal ingredients. Above all, be inspired and enjoy the preparation of these delicious recipes—it is easy to underestimate the uplifting effect that taking the time to cook for those closest to us, or even simply for oneself, can have.

fruit & oats

There's no better way to preserve the lusciousness of fruit than in a compote—and it's so easy to do. You can use any seasonal ripe fruit and it's lovely to have it all year round with muesli, porridge, or yogurt. Compote is also great served as a simple and light dessert after a rich meal. Experiment with combinations of your favorite fruits to make your own particular blend.

winter dried fruit pot

¾ cup dried apricots, pitted

¾ cup dates, pitted

¾ cup prunes, pitted

¾ cup golden raisins

1 cup dried blueberries

¼ cup dark brown sugar

serves 6

Put all the ingredients in a saucepan, add just enough water to cover, and stir. Cover with a lid, bring to a boil, and simmer for 30 minutes. Let cool, then transfer to a storage jar with a tight-fitting lid and refrigerate until needed.

rhubarb & plum compote

1 lb. rhubarb, chopped

1 lb. plums, pitted

1 inch fresh ginger, peeled and thinly sliced

⅓ cup sugar

serves 6

Put all the ingredients in a saucepan with ⅓ cup water, cover with a lid, and bring to a boil. Lower the heat and simmer for 5 minutes. Leave the lid on and set aside to cool. Transfer to a storage jar with a tight-fitting lid and refrigerate until needed.

apple & pear compote

1¼ lb. apples, peeled, cored, and chopped

1¼ lb. pears, peeled, cored, and chopped

¼ cup light brown sugar

1 vanilla bean, split lengthwise

serves 6

Put the fruit in a saucepan with 3 tablespoons water, then add the sugar and vanilla bean. Stir, cover with a lid, and bring to a boil. Lower the heat and simmer for 5 minutes. Leave the lid on and set aside to cool. Transfer to a storage jar with a tight-fitting lid and refrigerate until needed.

This is a simple fruit compote that is best served slightly warm. You can use nectarines instead of peaches if you prefer, plus whatever berries you fancy. It is complemented by thick, Greek yogurt and can even be served as a healthy dessert.

warm compote
with peaches, apricots, & blueberries

2 oranges

3 ripe peaches, pitted and sliced

8–12 apricots, pitted and halved

⅔ cup blueberries

2 tablespoons superfine sugar

1 cinnamon stick

Greek yogurt, to serve

serves 4

Grate the peel from 1 of the oranges, removing only the peel and not the bitter white pith. Cut the peel into thin strips and put in a shallow saucepan. Squeeze the juice from both oranges and add to the pan.

Add the peaches, apricots, blueberries, sugar, and cinnamon stick to the pan and heat gently until the sugar dissolves. Cover and simmer gently for 4–5 minutes, or until the fruits are softened.

Serve the compote warm with Greek yogurt.

There isn't much to beat figs straight from the tree, bursting with sweetness and a sublime flavor. Try to buy figs as ripe as possible for this dish. If they are unavailable, use other fruits such as peaches, apricots, or cherries.

fresh figs
with ricotta & honeycomb

1 lb. fresh ripe figs

1 lb. ricotta cheese, sliced

a piece of honeycomb or 4–8 tablespoons honey

serves 4

Arrange the figs and ricotta on a large plate and serve the honeycomb or honey in a separate bowl for everyone to help themselves.

Sometimes the best meals are the simplest—just fantastic fresh ingredients thrown together in no time. Everyone loves fruit, especially if it's all been prepared for them and looks stunning. This one is always a brunch winner.

fruit platter

1 ripe melon, such as orange cantaloupe or green honeydew

2 papayas

freshly squeezed juice of 2 limes

2½ cups mixed berries, such as blackberries, blueberries, raspberries, red currants, and strawberries

honey yogurt

2 cups Greek yogurt

⅓ cup clear honey

serves 4

Peel, halve, and seed the melon, then cut into wedges and slice. Divide between 4 plates. Peel, halve, seed, and cut the papaya into wedges. Add to the melon. Sprinkle with the lime juice, then add the berries.

Dollop the yogurt next to the fruit and drizzle with the honey.

Calcium is vital for healthy teeth and bones, and eating yogurt is a great way of getting enough. Teaming yogurt with fresh fruit is an ideal way to start the day. Look into making your own in a special yogurt machine if you want to avoid store-bought varieties, which often contain added sugar.

plum & honey cup

1¼ lb. plums, pitted

2 tablespoons honey

¾ cup plain yogurt

¾ cup mascarpone cheese

serves 4

Put the plums in a saucepan with the honey and 3 tablespoons water. Bring to a boil over medium heat, then cover and simmer very gently for about 8 minutes. Let cool.

Mix the yogurt and mascarpone together. Half-fill 4 glasses with this mixture, then top with the plums.

frozen berry yogurt cup

18 oz. frozen mixed berries

½ cup unrefined superfine sugar

2 cups Greek yogurt

serves 4

Put the frozen berries in a blender with the sugar and blitz into small pieces. Take 4 glasses and fill with alternating layers of yogurt and berries. Set aside for 5 minutes before serving.

banana & granola yogurt pot

1¾ cups plain yogurt

3 ripe bananas, sliced

⅓ cup pecans, roughly chopped

⅓ cup dark brown sugar

¾ cup House Granola (page 29)

1½ oz. semisweet chocolate, grated

serves 4

Divide the yogurt between 4 glasses. Top with the bananas, then add the pecans, sugar, granola, and chocolate.

Vanilla sugar is easy to make—just put a couple of vanilla beans in a jar of sugar and leave them there, topping up with fresh sugar as necessary. You can use the beans for cooking, pat dry with paper towels, then return them to the sugar.

roasted mascarpone peaches

4 large, ripe peaches

2 tablespoons clear honey

8 oz. mascarpone cheese

3 tablespoons vanilla sugar

1 vanilla bean, split lengthwise (optional)

1 tablespoon freshly squeezed lemon juice

serves 4

Preheat the oven to 400°F.

Cut the peaches in half, remove the pits, and arrange cut-side up in a roasting pan. Pour over the honey and bake in the preheated oven for about 20 minutes, or until softened and lightly golden.

Mix the mascarpone with the vanilla sugar and lemon juice. (If you want a stronger vanilla flavor, scrape the seeds from a vanilla bean into the mascarpone.) Spoon onto the hot peaches and serve.

Keep a big bowl of this compote in the refrigerator—it keeps well and is great with yogurt and a sprinkling of seeds. With lighter teas, use lighter-flavored fruits such as peaches and apples and flavor with lemon peel. Use orange peel to flavor stronger teas, together with stronger spices such as star anise. There is no need to add sugar, because the natural sugars from the fruits thicken the syrup as it cooks.

tea-infused
fruit compote

2 teaspoons leaf tea, such as Earl Grey or jasmine

1 lb. mixed dried fruit, such as prunes, apricots, or figs

1¼ cups apple juice

2 crushed cardamom pods

1 cinnamon stick

grated peel of 1 orange

serves 4

Make a large pot of tea with the leaf tea and 1 quart boiling water and set aside to brew. Put the fruit in a bowl and completely cover with the brewed tea. Cover and let soak for several hours or overnight.

Transfer to a saucepan, then add the apple juice, cardamom pods, cinnamon stick, and orange peel. Bring slowly to a boil, then reduce the heat and simmer for about 20 minutes until soft. Remove all the spices and let cool.

Cover and refrigerate for up to 1 week.

These kabobs are a great alternative to fruit salad. They work just as well cooked on a barbecue and served as a dessert in the summer. Feel free to experiment using your favorite fruits to get just the taste you like.

kickstart kabobs

2 small bananas, sliced

freshly squeezed juice of 1 lemon

8 cubes of canned pineapple in fruit juice, drained

1 large orange, peeled and divided into segments

8 dried prunes, pitted

8 dried apricots

2 tablespoons freshly squeezed orange juice

1 tablespoon clear honey

½ teaspoon apple pie spice

low-fat plain yogurt, to serve

4 long wooden skewers, soaked in water for 10 minutes

makes 4 kabobs

Put the bananas in a shallow bowl, sprinkle with the lemon juice, and toss gently to prevent them from browning. Thread the bananas, pineapple, orange, prunes, and apricots onto the skewers, dividing the ingredients equally between them.

Put the orange juice, honey, and apple pie spice in a small bowl and mix. Brush over the fruit skewers. Cook the kabobs under a medium-hot broiler for 5 minutes, turning frequently. Brush with any remaining orange juice mixture while they are cooking to prevent them from drying out. Serve warm, with some plain yogurt.

variation: Use other fresh, canned, or dried fruits of your choice, such as pink grapefruit, peaches, kiwi fruit, pears, and large raisins. Use pineapple or apple juice in place of the orange juice. Use ground cinnamon or nutmeg instead of the apple pie spice.

There are no limits to this breakfast indulgence, which can be made with any fruits you like. The top can be decorated as extravagantly as you dare using toasted shredded coconut, slivered almonds, or a purée of sieved raspberries, simply dribbled over the top.

exotic fruit scrunch

crispy oat scrunch

½ cup all-purpose or whole-wheat flour

1 cup whole rolled oats

4 tablespoons unsalted butter

¼ cup brown sugar

cream topping

1¼ cups heavy cream

¾ cup Greek yogurt

⅓ cup confectioners' sugar or to taste

exotic fruit layers

2 medium papayas (about 1 lb.), peeled, seeded, and sliced

1 large mango (about 1¼ lb.), peeled, seeded, and sliced

2 fresh figs, quartered

4 passion fruit

a 12 x 8-inch baking sheet, oiled

1 large glass serving bowl or 4 individual glasses

serves 4

Preheat the oven to 400°F.

To make the crispy oat scrunch, put the flour and oats in a medium bowl and mix well. Using your fingertips, rub in the butter until the mixture resembles bread crumbs. Stir in the sugar, then press the mixture firmly onto the prepared sheet. Bake in the preheated oven for 15 minutes, or until lightly golden. Let cool, then break it up into large random pieces.

To make the cream topping, whip the cream until soft peaks form. Stir in the yogurt and add confectioners' sugar, to taste.

Put the pieces of crispy oat scrunch in the bottom of 1 large bowl or 4 individual glasses, top with the papayas and mango, then the sweetened cream and yogurt mixture. Finish with some passion fruit flesh and the figs.

After tasting this, you will forget all other granolas and feel virtuous knowing that you made your own. What's more, with such a delicious and nutritious breakfast inside you, you'll be set for the rest of the day. You can store the cereal in an airtight container for up to 4 weeks—if it lasts that long!

house granola

4 cups rolled oats

⅓ cup whole almonds

⅓ cup raisins

5–6 dried apricots, chopped

⅓ cup pumpkin seeds

¼ cup raw sugar

4 tablespoons maple syrup

serves 4

Preheat the oven to 325°F.

Mix all the ingredients together in a large bowl, then transfer to a baking sheet. Bake in the preheated oven for 25 minutes, or until lightly toasted.

Remove from the oven and stir well. Return the mixture to the oven and cook for a further 15 minutes until the granola is crisp and light golden.

Remove from the oven. Serve hot or cold with milk.

What better way to start the day than with this soft Swiss-style muesli, steeped overnight in creamy yogurt, then served topped with delicious summer berries and honey. Packed with goodness and a joy to eat before facing the day.

swiss muesli

2⅔ cups rolled oats

1½ cups bran flakes

½ cup dried apple pieces

½ cup raisins

⅔ cup shredded coconut

½ cup chopped toasted hazelnuts

¼ cup sunflower seeds

450 ml plain yogurt

to serve

4 cups mixed fresh berries,
such as blueberries, raspberries,
and strawberries

4 tablespoons honey

serves 4

Mix all the dry ingredients in a large bowl. Add the yogurt, mix well, cover, and chill overnight.

Serve in bowls with a scattering of berries and the honey drizzled over the top.

These recipes make a hearty breakfast that will keep you feeling full well up to lunchtime. And research shows that oats can help lower your cholesterol, so they're healthy, too. Both the Extra Oaty Porridge and All-in-one Oats are packed with essential vitamins, minerals, and fiber.

extra oaty porridge

½ **cup rolled oats**

1 **tablespoon oat bran**

2¼ **cups skim milk, plus extra to serve (optional)**

2 **tablespoons golden raisins**

1 **banana, sliced**

2 **teaspoons honey or maple syrup**

1 **teaspoon slivered almonds**

makes 1 large serving

Put the oats, oat bran, and milk in a large microwaveable bowl and mix well. Cover and microwave on high for 4 minutes, stirring halfway through.

Alternatively, you can put the oats, oat bran, and milk in a saucepan and cook over medium heat for 5 minutes, stirring continuously.

Transfer to a serving bowl, add the golden raisins, banana, and extra milk, if using. Spoon over the honey, sprinkle with the almonds and serve.

variation: Replace the golden raisins with chopped dates or chopped dried figs and the almonds with finely chopped walnuts, hazelnuts, or brazil nuts. Add slices of kiwi fruit or peach instead of the banana, if you prefer.

all-in-one oats

base mixture

8 **tablespoons quick cooking rolled oats**

1 **tablespoon chopped dried apricots**

1 **tablespoon golden raisins**

1 **tablespoon finely chopped walnuts**

1 **tablespoon finely chopped almonds, brazil nuts, or hazelnuts**

to serve (per person)

½ **apple, grated**

¾–1¼ **cups skim milk**

4 **raspberries**

4 **blueberries**

4 **grapes**

½ **kiwi fruit, sliced**

1 **tablespoon plain yogurt (optional)**

serves 4

Put the oats, dried apricots, golden raisins, and nuts in an airtight container, shake well and reserve.

The night before you want to serve this for breakfast, pour about 3 tablespoons of the mixture into a large bowl. Add the grated apple and ¾ cup milk. Stir well.

Cover and refrigerate overnight. Just before serving, add a little more milk to loosen the mixture, if you like. Add the raspberries, blueberries, grapes, and kiwi fruit. Serve topped with plain yogurt, if using.

These lovely chewy bars are made with a basic mixture of butter, honey, sugar, oats, flour, and baking powder. You can add your own favorite dried fruits, seeds, and nuts or you could replace the nuts with chopped dates, dried figs, or dried cranberries.

muesli bars

7 tablespoons unsalted butter

⅓ cup clear honey

2 tablespoons light brown sugar

3½ cups rolled oats

2 tablespoons all-purpose flour

½ teaspoon baking powder

⅓ cup dried apricots, chopped

2 tablespoons sunflower seeds

2 tablespoons sesame seeds

2 tablespoons raisins

3 oz. mixed nuts or dried fruit and nut mix, chopped

an 8 x 10-inch baking pan, oiled and lined with baking parchment

makes 16 bars

Preheat the oven to 325°F.

Put the butter, honey, and sugar in a large saucepan over low heat. Heat gently until the butter melts, then remove from the heat. Stir gently with a wooden spoon. Tip the remaining ingredients into the pan and stir well.

Transfer the mixture to the prepared baking pan and spread evenly. Bake in the preheated oven for 30 minutes, or until golden brown. Remove the pan from the oven and put it on a wire rack. Let cool completely.

Run a round-bladed knife inside the edge of the pan, then invert onto a cutting board so the muesli mixture falls out in one piece. Cut into 16 bars. Store in an airtight container for up to 1 week.

sweet treats

This is the all-American classic, loved by millions for those lazy weekend mornings. You can use fresh or frozen berries, but frozen blueberries take slightly longer to cook and therefore don't burn so quickly.

blueberry sour cream pancakes
with maple syrup pecans

1½ cups all-purpose flour

2 teaspoons baking powder

1 teaspoon salt

¼ cup superfine sugar

2 eggs, separated

1 cup sour cream

⅔ cup milk

4 tablespoons unsalted butter, melted and cooled

8 oz. blueberries, fresh or frozen

vanilla ice cream, to serve

maple syrup pecans

4 oz. pecans

1 cup maple syrup

4 tablespoons unsalted butter

makes 8–10 pancakes

Preheat the oven to 400°F.

To make the maple syrup pecans, spread the pecan halves over a baking sheet and cook in the preheated oven for 5 minutes until lightly toasted. Simmer the maple syrup in a small saucepan for 3 minutes. Remove from the heat and stir in the pecans and butter.

To make the pancakes, sift the flour, baking powder, salt, and sugar into a bowl. Put the egg yolks, sour cream, milk, and butter into a second bowl and beat well, then add the flour mixture all at once and beat until smooth. Put the egg whites into a clean bowl and beat until soft peaks form. Fold them gently into the batter, then fold in the blueberries. (Do not overmix— a few lumps of flour and egg white don't matter.)

Lightly grease a skillet and preheat over medium heat. Reduce the heat. Pour 3 tablespoons of batter into the pan and cook in batches of 3–4 for 1–2 minutes over very low heat to avoid burning the blueberries, until small bubbles begin to appear on top and the underside is golden brown. Turn them over and cook the other side for 1 minute. Transfer to a plate and keep them warm in a low oven while you cook the remainder.

Serve with ice cream and the maple syrup pecans.

These pretty speckled pancakes are a treat. Orange zest gives the recipe a fresh edge while the poppyseeds provide a little crunch. Beware of the honey—too much and the pancakes will brown too quickly without giving the center enough time to cook.

poppyseed pancakes
with spiced clementines

4 clementines or small oranges

1 cup all-purpose flour

½ teaspoon baking powder

½ teaspoon baking soda

2½ tablespoons soft brown sugar

⅓ cup poppyseeds

1 egg

1 tablespoon honey

⅓ cup sour cream

⅓ cup milk

8 oz. mascarpone cheese, to serve

spiced sugar (makes 1 lb. 5 oz.)

3 cups firmly-packed brown sugar

2 cinnamon sticks, broken, plus 2 sticks to store

1 teaspoon allspice berries

1 teaspoon whole cloves

finely grated zest of 1 lemon

makes 10–12 small pancakes

To make the spiced sugar, put the brown sugar in a food processor, add the broken cinnamon sticks, allspice, cloves, and lemon zest and grind to a coarse powder. Sift through a wide-meshed sieve and discard any large pieces of spice. Store the spiced sugar in an airtight container with 2 cinnamon sticks.

To make the spiced clementines, grate the zest of 2 of the fruit, then peel all 4, removing as much of the bitter white pith as possible. Using a sharp knife, finely slice the fruit crosswise. Arrange the fruit on a plate, sprinkle with 4 tablespoons of the spiced sugar and set aside to infuse.

To make the pancakes, sift the flour, baking powder and baking soda in a large bowl, then stir in the soft brown sugar and poppyseeds.

Put the egg, honey, sour cream, and milk into a second large bowl, then add the reserved grated zest of the clementines. Beat well, then add the flour mixture all at once and keep beating until just smooth.

Lightly grease a stove-top grill pan or skillet and warm over over medium heat. Reduce the heat. Pour 1 tablespoon of batter into the pan and cook the pancakes in batches of 3–4 for 1 minute over low heat, until small bubbles begin to appear on the surface and the underside is golden brown. Turn the pancakes over and cook the other side for 1 minute. Transfer to a plate and keep them warm in a low oven while you cook the remainder.

To serve, layer the poppyseed pancakes with slices of clementines and spoonfuls of mascarpone.

Some mornings are made for indulgence. When complete chocolate overload is called for, make these pancakes. Packed with velvety melted chocolate and finished with the sweet-and-sour taste of smooth white chocolate yogurt.

triple chocolate pancakes

1½ cups all-purpose flour

¾ cup cocoa powder

1 teaspoon baking powder

1 teaspoon baking soda

¼ superfine sugar

¾ cup milk

½ cup buttermilk

2 eggs, separated

3 tablespoons unsalted butter, melted and cooled

½ teaspoon salt

3 oz. bittersweet chocolate, chopped

3 oz. white chocolate, chopped

ready-made chocolate sauce, to serve (optional)

white chocolate yogurt

6 oz. white chocolate

4 tablespoons Greek yogurt

makes about 12 pancakes

Sift the flour, cocoa, baking powder, baking soda, and sugar into a bowl. Put the milk, buttermilk, egg yolks, and butter into a second large bowl and beat well. Add the flour mixture and mix thoroughly.

Put the egg whites and salt into a clean bowl and beat until stiff peaks form. Add 1 tablespoon of the egg whites to the pancake mixture and stir to loosen it, then carefully fold in the remaining egg whites, then the bittersweet and white chocolate.

Lightly grease a stove-top grill-pan or skillet and warm over medium heat. Reduce the heat. Pour about 2 tablespoons of batter into the pan and cook in batches of 3–4 over low heat for about 1 minute, or until small bubbles begin to appear on the surface and the underside is golden brown. Turn the pancakes over and cook the other side for 1 minute.

Transfer to a plate and keep them warm in a low oven while you cook the remainder. To make the white chocolate yogurt, put the chocolate into a bowl set over a saucepan of simmering water and melt slowly. Remove from the heat and leave to cool a little, then beat in the yogurt until the mixture is smooth and shiny. Serve with the pancakes and hot chocolate sauce, if using.

Adding sliced fruit to the top of any pancake turns it into something special and these apple-topped griddle cakes are no exception. Some fruits burn more quickly than others, so keep a close watch on the cakes while they are cooking.

date & pistachio griddle cakes

1½ cups all-purpose flour

2 teaspoons baking powder

1 teaspoon salt

3 tablespoons light brown sugar

⅔ cup rolled oats

4 oz. shelled, unsalted pistachio nuts, coarsely chopped

4 oz. dates, pitted and finely chopped

1 cup milk

2 eggs

4 tablespoons unsalted butter, melted and cooled, plus extra for brushing

grated zest of 1 lemon

2 apples

to serve

fresh honeycomb (optional)

Greek yogurt or sour cream

makes 12 griddle cakes

Sift the flour, baking powder, and salt into a large bowl, then stir in the sugar, oats, nuts, and dates. Put the milk, eggs, butter, and lemon zest into another bowl, beat well, then add the nut and oat mixture and stir gently. (Be careful not to overwork the mixture—it doesn't matter if the dough isn't smooth.)

Before you begin to cook the griddle cakes, prepare the apple by slicing it horizontally into ⅛-inch rings and removing the core of each slice with a cookie cutter (a star shape works best).

Lightly grease a stove-top griddle or skillet over medium heat. Reduce the heat. Pour 1 tablespoon of batter onto the griddle and top with an apple slice. Cook in batches of 3–4 for 2–3 minutes over low heat, or until small bubbles begin to appear on the surface and the underside is golden brown. Brush the apple slice with a little melted butter, then turn the pancakes over and cook the other side for about 2 minutes. Repeat until all the mixture and apple slices have been used. Transfer to a plate and keep them warm in a low oven while you cook the remainder.

Serve immediately with honeycomb, if using, and Greek yogurt.

This recipe has lovely Fall associations. Allspice is the secret ingredient—it brings all the fruit and nut flavors together, and grinding your own allspice berries—in a dedicated pepper grinder—will make sure you get the full force of the spice.

apple whole-wheat waffles
with sugar plums

1½ cups all-purpose flour

½ cup whole-wheat flour

2 teaspoons baking powder

½ teaspoon salt

2 tablespoons brown sugar

1 teaspoon ground allspice

2 oz. pecans, chopped

2 eggs, separated

¾ cup milk

1 tablespoon molasses

4 tablespoons unsalted butter, melted and cooled

2 crisp apples, peeled, cored, and coarsely chopped

sugar plums

6 ripe plums, quartered and pitted

4 oz. spiced sugar (page 41)

2 tablespoons unsalted butter

freshly squeezed juice of ½ lemon

a deep Belgian waffle iron

makes 8 deep Belgian-size waffles

To make the sugar plums, put the quartered plums and spiced sugar into a bowl and toss to coat. Melt the butter in a small skillet over medium heat until it foams, then add all the plum pieces and gently sauté until caramelized. Add the lemon juice to loosen the butter syrup and set aside to keep warm while you prepare the waffles.

Lightly grease the waffle iron and preheat. To make the waffles, put the all-purpose and whole-wheat flours into a large bowl, add the baking powder, salt, sugar, allspice, and pecans and stir well.

Put the egg yolks into another bowl, add the milk, molasses, and butter and beat well. Add the flour mixture, stir well, then stir in the chopped apple. Put the egg whites into a clean, grease-free bowl and beat until stiff peaks form, then fold gently into the waffle batter with a metal spoon.

Spoon about ½ cup of the batter into the preheated waffle iron compartments, making sure each batch has lots of apple in it. Adjust the amount of batter according to the size of your iron. Cook until crisp, about 3–5 minutes. The waffles should be crisp on the outside and served immediately. At a pinch, they can be kept warm in a low oven, but will lose some crispness. A quick reheating in the toaster works remarkably well.

Serve the waffles immediately, topped with warm plums and plenty of sticky plum juice.

Belgian waffles are traditionally thick, with deep wells to trap butter and syrup. The best use a yeast-raised batter and it's definitely worth the effort. By doing the hard work the night before, all you need to do in the morning is add the eggs and bake.

classic belgian waffles
with strawberries & praline cream

2 cups all-purpose flour

2 tablespoons superfine sugar

1 teaspoon salt

1 teaspoon active dry yeast

1½ sticks unsalted butter, melted and cooled

1½ cups milk

1 teaspoon vanilla extract

3 eggs, separated

8 oz. strawberries, to serve

praline cream

1¼ cups heavy cream

2 oz. store-bought hazelnut brittle, ground to a powder in a spice grinder

a deep Belgian waffle iron

makes 12 waffles

Start the night before. Sift the flour, sugar, salt, and yeast into a large bowl. Stir in the butter, milk, and vanilla extract to make a smooth mixture. Cover the bowl with plastic wrap and leave at room temperature overnight.

First thing in the morning, lightly grease the waffle iron and preheat. Beat the egg yolks into the yeast mixture. Put the egg whites into a clean, grease-free bowl and beat with a wire whisk until stiff peaks form. Carefully fold them into the batter with a metal spoon.

To make the praline cream, put the cream into a clean bowl and whip to a soft, loose consistency. Stir in the ground hazelnut brittle.

Pour about ½ cup batter into the preheated waffle iron compartments. Adjust the amount of batter according to the size of your iron. Cook until golden, 3–5 minutes. The waffles should be crisp on the outside and served immediately. In a pinch, they can be kept warm in a low oven, but will lose some crispness. A quick reheating in the toaster works remarkably well.

Serve the waffles hot with a spoonful of the praline cream and a few fresh strawberries.

These delicate waffles are jam-packed with fruit. As the batter cooks, the raspberries soften and the juice seeps into the fabric of the waffle giving a beautiful red mottled effect. Sour cream on the side will counteract the delicious sweetness of the honey.

raspberry waffles
with peach & pistachio honey

1½ cups all-purpose flour

2 teaspoons baking powder

½ teaspoon salt

3 tablespoons superfine sugar

3 eggs, separated

1 cup milk

4 tablespoons unsalted butter, melted and cooled

2 teaspoons vanilla extract

6 oz. fresh raspberries

sour cream, to serve (optional)

peach & pistachio honey

2 firm peaches, skinned and pitted

1½ cups clear orange-blossom honey

1 tablespoon peach schnapps (optional)

2 oz. shelled unsalted pistachios

a waffle iron

makes 8 waffles

To make the peach and pistachio honey, cut the peaches into ⅛-inch cubes. Put the honey and schnapps, if using, in a saucepan and heat until almost boiling. Remove the pan from the heat, add the chopped peaches and the pistachios and leave to cool slightly.

Lightly grease the waffle iron and preheat. To make the waffles, sift the flour, baking powder, salt, and sugar in a large bowl. Put the egg yolks, milk, butter, and vanilla extract in a separate bowl and beat well. Add the dry ingredients to the egg mixture and stir until just mixed. Add the raspberries to the batter, crushing some with the back of a spoon to give a marbled effect.

Put the egg whites in a clean, grease-free bowl and beat with a wire whisk until stiff peaks form. Gently fold them into the waffle batter using a large metal spoon.

Spoon 4–8 tablespoons of batter into each preheated compartment. Adjust the amount of batter according to the size of your iron. Cook until golden, about 4–5 minutes. The waffles should be crisp on the outside and served immediately. In a pinch, they can be kept warm in a low oven, but will lose some crispness. A quick reheating in the toaster works remarkably well.

Serve the waffles warm, topped with a spoonful of the peach and pistachio honey and some sour cream, if using.

Doughnuts have long made a quick and substantial fresh breakfast and this remains true today, especially in America. This is based on an old Irish settler recipe and uses mashed floury potatoes for speed and flavor. The spices make it an absolute winner.

breakfast doughnuts

3 cups all-purpose flour

¼ teaspoon sea salt

½ teaspoon ground ginger

½ teaspoon ground cinnamon

½ teaspoon freshly grated nutmeg

1½ teaspoons baking soda

1 cup raw sugar

3 tablespoons unsalted butter, diced

1 cup very smooth mashed potatoes

2 eggs, beaten

1 cup buttermilk (or a mixture of half plain yogurt and half 2% fat milk)

vegetable oil, for deep-frying

cinnamon sugar

2 tablespoons superfine sugar

1 teaspoon ground cinnamon

a deep-fat fryer

makes 12 doughnuts

Mix the flour with the salt, spices, baking soda, and sugar in a large bowl. Rub in the butter using the tips of your fingers until the mixture resembles coarse bread crumbs.

Add the mashed potatoes, mix briefly, then add the eggs and enough of the buttermilk to make a soft dough. If the dough feels very sticky, add extra flour 1 tablespoon at a time.

Turn out the dough onto a lightly floured work surface and knead for a few seconds until it is just smooth. Roll it out ½-inch thick, then cut out rounds using an 3-inch round cookie cutter (or upturned glass.) Stamp out the center of each round with a 1-inch round cookie cutter. Re-roll the trimmings and center circles, then cut out more rings.

Fill a deep-fat fryer with vegetable oil to the manufacturer's recommended level. Heat the oil to 350°F, or until a cube of bread browns in about 40 seconds. Fry the doughnuts 2 or 3 at a time, turning them frequently until well browned and cooked through, about 4 minutes. Remove from the oil with a slotted spoon and drain well on paper towels.

Mix the cinnamon sugar ingredients together, sprinkle over the doughnuts, then serve warm with coffee. They are best eaten within 24 hours.

Dream of Seville, Madrid, and Barcelona when you eat these doughnuts. Serve with hot chocolate and it will complete the illusion. It is essential to cook the extruded batter in very hot olive oil, to crisp and seal the outside and steam the batter inside.

churros
with hot chocolate

5 cups self-rising flour

½ teaspoon salt

1 egg, beaten

2 cups milk

light olive oil, for deep-frying

½ cup superfine sugar

¼ cup ground cinnamon (optional)

hot chocolate

9 oz. bittersweet chocolate, chopped or grated

2½ cups milk, boiled

a pastry bag fitted with a ½–1 inch plain nozzle

serves 4

Sift the flour and salt in a bowl and make a well in the center. Beat the egg in a bowl with 1 cup of the milk. Pour into the well and beat into the flour. Gradually beat in enough of the remaining milk to make a smooth, creamy, thick batter able to be piped easily. Transfer to the pastry bag.

Pour a 4-inch depth of olive oil into a heavy-bottomed saucepan fitted with a frying basket. Heat the oil to 375°F, or until a cube of bread browns in 35 seconds.

Pipe long, spiraled, coiled-up lengths of batter directly into the oil. Leave to sizzle and cook for 4–6 minutes, or until golden and spongy in the center (test one to check.)

Lift the churros out of the oil using the basket or tongs. Drain on crumpled paper towels. Repeat using the remaining doughnut mixture.

When cool, scissor-snip the churros into 6-inch lengths. Put the superfine sugar in a plate, mix in the cinnamon, if using, then roll the churros in the mixture.

To make the hot chocolate, mix the chocolate and boiled milk together in a small saucepan, beating and cooking until the chocolate is well blended and the liquid is dusky brown. Serve in 4 cups or bowls with the churros.

These corn cakes are eaten at street fairs, bars, and markets all over Colombia and Venezuela. Arepa meal (*masarepa*), sold in gourmet stores or Hispanic markets, is a ready-cooked flour made from very starchy cooked corn.

arepas
yellow corn cakes with fruit batidas

1½ cups fresh or frozen corn kernels

1¼ cups yellow arepa meal (*masarepa*) or semolina

1¼ cups grated white cheese, such as Mexican *queso fresco* or mozzarella

1¼ cups grated yellow cheese, such as Monterey Jack or cheddar

1 teaspoon baking powder

½ teaspoon salt

3 tablespoons superfine sugar

2 fresh serrano or jalapeño chiles, seeded and chopped

6 tablespoons milk

corn oil, for brushing

fresh fruit batida

assorted tropical fruit, such as mango, guava, melon, and papaya

sugar syrup, to taste

makes 18 arepas

To make the fresh fruit batida, peel and pit (where necessary) your choice of tropical fruit. Put through a juicer or purée in a blender. Add sugar syrup to taste, plus crushed ice and mineral water if necessary.

To make the arepas, process the sweetcorn kernels in a food processor until fine. Transfer to a bowl, then mix in the arepa meal, the two cheeses, baking powder, salt, sugar, and chiles. Mix the milk with 1 tablespoon hot water, stir into the flour mixture and mix to a stiff dough. Divide into 18 portions, roll into balls, and flatten into patties about ½ inch thick.

Preheat a stove-top grill pan or skillet, brush with oil, add the arepas, in batches and cook over low to medium heat for 3 minutes on each side, until golden and crusty outside and soft inside.

Serve with the fresh fruit batida and a cup of strong black coffee.

For many of us, French toast conjures up comforting memories of childhood. Why not recreate that nostalgia next time you have a few minutes to spare on a weekend morning? The most important thing is to use premium ingredients—the best white bread (or even brioche), the creamiest unsalted butter, and finest ground cinnamon.

french toast

4 slices thick-cut white bread, brioche or challah

2 large eggs, beaten

2 tablespoons light cream

½ teaspoon vanilla extract

3½ tablespoons raw sugar

2 tablespoons unsalted butter, for frying

½ teaspoon ground cinnamon

maple syrup, to serve (optional)

serves 4

Trim the crusts from the bread, then cut the slices in half. Put the eggs, cream, vanilla extract, and 1 teaspoon of the sugar in a shallow dish and mix with a fork.

Heat half the butter in a large, heavy, nonstick skillet. When the butter is foaming, thoroughly coat a piece of bread in the egg mixture, drain off the excess and put it in the hot butter. Add 3 more pieces of coated bread to the skillet in the same way, then cook over medium heat for 3–4 minutes until the underside is golden brown. Turn over and cook the other side. Meanwhile, mix the remaining sugar and cinnamon in a small sugar shaker or bowl. Put the cooked bread on a warm serving plate and sprinkle with some of the cinnamon sugar.

Wipe out the skillet, reheat and cook the remaining pieces of bread as before. Serve hot, sprinkled with more cinnamon sugar and maple syrup, if using.

variation: To make cinnamon toast, heat the broiler, toast thick slices of bread on both sides, then butter thoroughly. Mix the cinnamon sugar as in the recipe above, and sprinkle generously to cover. Put the toast back under the broiler until the sugar starts to melt and bubble. Remove carefully and eat when the toast has cooled enough not to burn your lips (the top will look like a brandy snap—lacy and crisp.)

Somewhere between a light and fluffy bread-and-butter pudding and an unbelievably moist French toast, this is a divine concoction. Panettone is a sweet yeast bread traditionally eaten at Christmas in Italy.

creamy orange french toast

¼ cup light cream

2 large egg yolks

freshly grated zest of ½ an orange

2 teaspoons freshly squeezed orange juice

1 teaspoon sugar

1 tablespoon unsalted butter

2 thick slices of panettone, cut in half

confectioners' sugar, to dust

strips of orange zest, to decorate

orange cream

3 tablespoons sour cream

1 teaspoon confectioners' sugar

1 tablespoon freshly squeezed orange juice

½ teaspoon freshly squeezed lemon juice

serves 2

To make the orange cream, put the sour cream, confectioners' sugar, orange juice, and lemon juice in a bowl and stir until smooth and creamy. Set aside until needed.

Put the cream, egg yolks, grated orange zest, and juice and the sugar in a wide, shallow dish and beat well. Heat the butter in a large, non-stick skillet. Dip each slice of panettone in the custard mixture, coating each side well, then arrange in the skillet. Spoon any remaining custard mixture over the toasts and fry for 2 minutes, or until golden underneath.

Very carefully flip the toasts over and cook for a further 1–2 minutes until golden. Put 2 slices of French toast on each plate, then dust with confectioners' sugar, drizzle over the orange cream and top with strips of orange zest.

Using coconut milk instead of regular milk and Italian panettone instead of bread adds a mouth-watering twist to this simple breakfast dish. For a slightly healthier version, you can serve it with yogurt instead of cream.

panettone french toast
with coconut milk

½ **vanilla bean**

⅔ **cup canned coconut milk**

2 **eggs, lightly beaten**

2 **tablespoons superfine sugar**

¼ **teaspoon ground cardamom (optional)**

4 **tablespoons unsalted butter**

8 **slices of panettone or other sweet bread**

to serve

confectioners' sugar, to dust

blueberries

heavy or whipped cream

serves 4

Split the vanilla bean in half lengthways and scrape out the seeds. Put the coconut milk, eggs, sugar, vanilla seeds, and cardamom, if using, in a bowl and beat well. Pour the mixture into a shallow dish.

Heat half the butter in a large skillet. Dip 2 slices of panettone into the egg mixture and sauté until golden on both sides, about 2 minutes for each side. Repeat with the remaining slices and serve dusted with confectioners' sugar and topped with the blueberries and whipped cream.

This luscious toast is like a free-form summer pudding or an indulgent trifle, with the sweet, alcoholic juices soaking into the brioche and the rich, creamy mascarpone sliding off the top. You can use any combination of summer berries, but I like strawberries and blueberries the best.

macerated berries
on brioche french toast

1 cup strawberries, hulled

⅓ cup blueberries

1 teaspoon sugar

2½ tablespoons Grand Marnier

3 tablespoons mascarpone cheese

1 tablespoon confectioners' sugar

2 thick slices of brioche

fresh mint leaves, to serve (optional)

serves 2

Halve or quarter the strawberries, depending on size, and put in a bowl with the blueberries. Sprinkle with the sugar, then add the Grand Marnier and leave to macerate for at least 1 hour.

Just before serving, put the mascarpone and confectioners' sugar in a bowl and stir in 2–3 teaspoons of the macerating juices from the berries.

Lightly toast the brioche on both sides, then spread with a thick layer of mascarpone and spoon the macerated berries and all the juices on top. Top with fresh mint leaves, if using, and serve immediately.

Quince paste (Spanish *membrillo*) is available from gourmet stores and the deli counter of some supermarkets, and is worth seeking out for its distinctive flavor. As an alternative, you can also use raspberry preserve or redcurrant jelly.

sweet bruschetta
with quince-glazed figs

2 tablespoons quince paste

2 tablespoons butter

2 tablespoons port

12 ripe figs, halved

4 slices of brioche or challah

confectioners' sugar and cinnamon, to dust

Greek yogurt, to serve

serves 4

Put the quince paste, butter, and port in a saucepan and heat gently until melted. Arrange the figs, cut-side up, in an ovenproof dish. Spoon over the port mixture, making sure the surface of each fig is well covered.

Put under a hot broiler and cook for 3–5 minutes, until the figs are caramelized and heated through.

Meanwhile, toast the brioche in a stove-top grill pan. Transfer to warmed serving plates and sprinkle with confectioners' sugar and cinnamon. Top with the figs and serve with Greek yogurt.

This is the ultimate in no-fuss indulgence. For best results, choose a really good lemon curd and a thick, mild-tasting yogurt. Check the flavor of the lemon cream once you've mixed it up—if you use a bland lemon curd, you may have to add a little extra.

toasted brioche
with lemon cream & fresh raspberries

½ cup sour cream

½ cup plain yogurt

3–4 tablespoons lemon curd

3–4 individual brioche buns or 6–8 thick slices of brioche

1½ cups fresh raspberries

confectioners' sugar, to dust (optional)

serves 3–4

Put the sour cream, yogurt, and lemon curd in a bowl and mix briefly. Set aside.

Cut the brioche buns in half and lightly toast under a hot broiler. Arrange the base of each brioche on a plate, spoon the lemon cream mixture on top, then pile on the raspberries.

Add the toasted lid, dust with confectioners' sugar, if using, and serve immediately.

big bites

Cheese on toast has always been a popular comfort food, so what better way start your weekend than with an oozing cheese waffle on which to build your favorite brunch. Most cheeses—from cottage cheese to cheddar to Parmesan—will work.

morning-after
breakfast waffles

¾ **cup plus 2 tablespoons all-purpose flour**

¾ **cup fine cornmeal**

2 teaspoons baking powder

½ **teaspoon sea salt**

2 eggs, separated

1 cup milk

¾ **cup sour cream or yogurt**

2 tablespoons olive oil, plus extra for frying and roasting

4 oz. cheddar cheese, grated

2 tablespoons snipped fresh chives

to serve

20 cherry tomatoes, on the vine

16 bacon slices

8 eggs

sea salt and freshly ground black pepper

a waffle iron

makes 8 waffles

Preheat the oven to 400°F and grease a baking sheet. Lightly grease and preheat the waffle iron.

Put the vine tomatoes on the prepared baking sheet, sprinkle with olive oil, season and roast for 5 minutes or until their skins blister.

To make the waffles, sift the flour, cornmeal, baking powder, and salt in a large bowl. Put the egg yolks into another bowl, add the milk, sour cream and olive oil and beat well. Add the flour mixture and beat well. Put the egg whites in a clean bowl and beat until stiff peaks form. Using a large metal spoon, gently fold the egg whites, cheddar and chives into the batter.

Brush a small skillet with olive oil and heat well. Add the bacon and fry until crisp. Remove from the skillet and leave to drain on paper towels. Brush the skillet with oil again, add 4 slices of the cooked bacon, then break 2 eggs on top and fry gently until the eggs are done. Set aside to keep warm.

Spoon about ¼–½ cup of the batter into the preheated waffle iron compartments. Adjust the amount of batter according to the size of your iron. Cook until crisp, at least 4–5 minutes (cheese waffles taste so much better when well done.) Transfer to a large plate, slide the bacon and eggs on top and serve with the tomatoes. Repeat to make the other servings.

This dish makes a good breakfast when you're feeling a little the worse for wear—it is great comfort food and is sure to fill you up. Choose a good baking potato, such as russets, to ensure the perfect texture for the hash browns.

hash browns
with sausages & oven-roasted tomatoes

1½ lb. potatoes, diced

4 tablespoons butter

1 large onion, finely chopped

12 premium breakfast sausages

2 tablespoons olive oil

20 cherry tomatoes, on the vine

1 tablespoon balsamic vinegar

sea salt and freshly ground black pepper

serves 4

Preheat the oven to 400°F. Lightly grease a baking sheet.

Cook the potatoes in a large saucepan of lightly salted boiling water for 10–12 minutes, until almost cooked through. Drain and mash roughly.

Melt the butter in a large, nonstick skillet and gently fry the onion for 15 minutes, until soft and golden. Add the potatoes and seasoning. Cook, stirring and mashing the potatoes occasionally, for about 15–20 minutes, or until well browned and crispy around the edges.

Meanwhile, put the sausages in a roasting pan, drizzle with half the oil, and roast on the middle shelf of the preheated oven for 25 minutes.

Once the sausages are in the oven, put the vine tomatoes on the prepared baking sheet. Drizzle with the remaining oil and put on the top shelf of the oven after the sausages have been cooking for 5 minutes. Cook for about 15 minutes, then drizzle over the balsamic vinegar and cook for a further 5 minutes.

Spoon the hash browns onto plates and top with the sausages, tomatoes, and their juices.

Great for breakfast, but just as good for brunch, lunch, a mid-afternoon snack, or midnight feast, this winning combination of toasted croissant, melting Gruyère, wafer-thin slices of ham, and juicy fresh peaches can't be beaten.

melting cheese & ham croissants

1 teaspoon grainy mustard

1 teaspoon balsamic vinegar

1 tablespoon olive oil

2 slices of prosciutto or other wafer-thin cured ham, about 1 oz.

½ ripe peach

2 croissants

2 large slices of Swiss cheese, such as Gruyère or Emmental, about 2 oz.

serves 2

Put the mustard, vinegar, and oil in a bowl, mix well, then set aside. Cut the ham slices in half lengthwise to make 4 long strips. Slice the peach into thin wedges.

Split the croissants in half and arrange on a broiler pan, cut-side down. Cook under a hot broiler for about 2 minutes until very lightly toasted, then flip over and fold a slice of cheese on the bottom half of each one. Broil until the cheese is melting, and the top halves are golden. (The top halves will be done just before the cheese-covered halves, so remove and keep them warm.)

Arrange the ham and peach wedges over the melting cheese, drizzle over the dressing, top with the second half of the croissant and serve.

When you require both style and substance first thing, make these breakfast kabobs. Visually impressive thanks to the tomatoes, bell peppers, and onions, and protein-packed, you'll be set up for the day. The onion can be replaced with a large, flat field mushroom.

breakfast kabobs

½ **red bell pepper**

½ **green bell pepper**

½ **yellow bell pepper**

4 **back bacon slices**

1 **small red onion**

8 **cherry tomatoes or baby plum tomatoes**

8 **small cocktail sausages**

4 **soft whole-wheat rolls or pita breads**

4 wooden skewers, soaked in warm water for 10 minutes

makes 4 kabobs

Preheat the oven to 425°F and grease a large roasting pan.

Seed the peppers then cut them into large chunks. Cut each slice of bacon in half, then roll up. Cut the onion into quarters. Leave the tomatoes and sausages whole.

Thread the bell peppers, bacon, onion, tomatoes, and sausages onto the wooden skewers, leaving a small gap between each piece on the skewer. Put them in any order you like, but make sure each skewer has an equal amount of each ingredient.

Arrange the kabobs in the prepared roasting pan, slightly apart. Bake for 15–20 minutes, or until golden. Meanwhile, warm the bread rolls, either in the toaster or in a second oven on a low temperature. Put a kabob on each serving plate and serve immediately with the warmed bread.

You can keep any of this lovely leftover garlic mayonnaise covered and refrigerated for up to three days. Both it and the caramelized shallots are very good served with many other dishes. Try the shallots with sausages, and the mayonnaise with fries or baked potatoes.

mushroom burgers
with caramelized shallots & garlic mayonnaise

4 large portobello mushrooms

1 tablespoon extra virgin olive oil

4 large ciabatta rolls

sea salt and freshly ground black pepper

mixed salad greens, to serve

caramelized shallots

1 tablespoon extra virgin olive oil

4½ oz. shallots, thinly sliced

2 tablespoons redcurrant jelly

1 tablespoon red wine vinegar

garlic mayonnaise

1 egg yolk

1 garlic clove, peeled and crushed

1 teaspoon freshly squeezed lemon juice

a pinch of sea salt

¼ pint light olive oil

serves 4

To make the caramelized shallots, heat the olive oil in a small skillet and cook the shallots for 15 minutes. Add 1 tablespoon water, the redcurrant jelly, and the vinegar. Cook for a further 10–15 minutes, or until reduced and thickened. Season to taste and let cool.

To make the mayonnaise, put the egg yolk, garlic, lemon juice, and salt in a bowl and beat until blended. Gradually beat in the olive oil, a little at a time, until thickened and glossy.

Trim the mushrooms, brush all over with the olive oil and sprinkle with seasoning. Add to a hot nonstick skillet and cook for 4–5 minutes each side. Cut the ciabatta rolls in half and toast on a preheated stove-top grill pan. Put the mushrooms on 4 of the toasted ciabatta halves and top with caramelized shallots, mayonnaise and the remaining ciabatta halves. Serve with mixed salad.

There's nothing quite like a warm sausage-filled roll for brunch. Dotting the sausages with mustard and wrapping them in bacon just adds to the taste experience and the cooking smells will waken even the most sleepy.

sausage & bacon rolls

a little mustard (any kind)

16 thin slices of Italian pancetta or streaky bacon

8 premium breakfast sausages

olive oil, for brushing

to serve

4 warm buttered soft rolls or pita breads

tomato ketchup or broiled tomatoes

serves 4

Preheat the broiler to medium-hot. Spread a little mustard over each slice of bacon. Wrap 2 slices around each sausage. Put the sausages on the rack of a broiler pan so that the loose ends of the bacon are underneath the sausages.

Brush with a little olive oil. Cook under the preheated broiler for about 6–8 minutes on each side, depending on the thickness of the sausage, or until the bacon is crisp and the sausage cooked through. Serve in buttered rolls with plenty of tomato ketchup or broiled tomatoes.

Blini—little Russian pancakes—are usually made with buckwheat flour and topped with sour cream and caviar or smoked salmon. They are equally good made with mashed potato, then served with salty salmon and crème fraîche (French-style sour cream).

fluffy potato pancakes
with smoked salmon

1 lb. potatoes, such as russets

⅔ cup crème fraîche or sour cream

3 eggs, separated

¼ cup snipped fresh chives

4 tablespoons unsalted butter

sea salt and freshly ground black pepper

to serve

1 lb. sliced smoked salmon

1¼ cups crème fraîche or sour cream

1 small bunch of chives, snipped

4 blini pans or a nonstick skillet and 4 ring molds

serves 4

Boil the potatoes until tender, then drain. Mash, then beat in the cream and egg yolks. Season and beat in the chives.

Beat the egg whites in a clean, grease-free bowl until stiff but not dry and fold into the potatoes.

Heat 4 blini pans, or a nonstick skillet containing 4 ring molds. Add ½ tablespoon butter to each blini pan or 2 tablespoons to the skillet. When the butter is foaming, spoon in about 4 tablespoons of the mixture into each pan or ring mold. Cook until browning and set, then flip over and cook for 1 minute more. Remove from the pans to a kitchen towel and keep warm in the cloth. Repeat with the remaining butter and potato mixture it has all been used.

Serve the potato pancakes topped with crinkled smoked salmon, a dollop of crème fraîche, and some snipped chives.

Masa harina and chile give this recipe a slightly Mexican flavor. If you wish to continue this theme, try these pancakes with huevos rancheros or even avocado salsa. Otherwise, serve with fried portobello mushrooms, cherry tomatoes, and eggs.

cornmeal & bacon breakfast stack

⅔ cup all-purpose flour

1½ teaspoons baking powder

½ cup *masa harina* or fine yellow cornmeal

1 egg, separated

½ cup buttermilk

¾ cup milk

2 tablespoons freshly grated Parmesan cheese

6 oz. prosciutto or bacon, chopped

4 scallions, cut into ¼-inch slices

1 medium green chile, seeded and thinly sliced

sea salt and freshly ground black pepper

4 muffin rings, 3½ inches diameter, greased

makes 4 pancakes

Preheat the oven to 400°F. Lightly grease a flat grill pan or large skillet and warm over medium heat.

Sift the flour, baking powder, and 1 teaspoon salt in a large bowl, then stir in the *masa harina*. Put the egg yolks in another bowl, add the buttermilk and milk and beat well. Add the flour mixture and beat to a thick batter. Stir in the Parmesan. Put the egg white into a clean, grease-free bowl and beat until stiff peaks form, then fold into the batter using a metal spoon.

Add the prepared muffin rings to the grill pan or skillet and heat well. Divide the bacon between the 4 muffin rings and fry for 1 minute. Add a share of the scallions and chile, then add 2 tablespoons of the batter to each ring. When the mixture has risen and started to set, remove the rings. Turn the pancakes over and cook until brown. Transfer to a plate and keep them warm in a low oven until you're ready to serve.

Rösti are a Swiss classic. These soft buttery pancakes are usually topped with wild mushrooms but can also be served topped with fried eggs, sprinkled with Gruyère cheese or served separately with meat and sausages.

swiss rösti

2 lb. potatoes, unpeeled and well scrubbed

¾ cup clarified butter*

1 onion, chopped

4 oz. pancetta or smoked bacon, cut into thin strips

1 lb. wild or large, flat, cultivated mushrooms, or a mixture of both, cut in halves or quarters if large

2 tablespoons chopped fresh flat-leaf parsley

sea salt and freshly ground black pepper

serves 4

To clarify butter, melt over gentle heat, then let cool. Skim off the pure butter and discard the solids and water.

Put the potatoes in a large pan and cover with cold water. Bring to a boil and cook for 10–15 minutes, or until just tender. Drain well and leave to cool slightly. Peel, then grate coarsely into a large bowl.

Heat 2 tablespoons of the butter in a skillet, add the onion and pancetta and cook for 5–6 minutes, or until the onions are softened. Tip this mixture into the bowl of potato, season, and mix well.

Heat half the remaining butter in a skillet, add the potato mixture and press down slightly to form a large pancake. Cook for 10 minutes, adding a little extra butter around the edges and shaking the skillet occasionally.

Carefully cover the skillet with a large plate and flip over. Add more butter, then slide the rösti back in to cook the other side. Add butter around the edge and cook until golden, about 7 minutes. Remove from the heat and keep warm.

Heat the remaining butter in a skillet. Add the mushrooms and cook, stirring occasionally, for 3–5 minutes, or until tender but still firm. Season and stir in the chopped parsley. Serve the rösti with the mushrooms.

Almost everyone loves a bacon sandwich and this is a really healthy, quick, and easy version. The combination of hot tomato, fresh basil, and sizzling bacon makes a fabulous taste-sensation that is perfect for breakfast or brunch.

bacon, tomato & basil toasty

2 slices extra-lean bacon

1 tomato, sliced

1 thick slice of whole-grain bread

2 teaspoons chopped fresh basil

sea salt and freshly ground black pepper

serves 1

Put the bacon slices on a broiler pan and cook under a hot broiler for 2 minutes. Add the tomato slices to the pan and cook for a further 2 minutes. Turn the bacon over and add the slice of bread to the pan. Let the bread go golden brown on one side before turning over and lightly toasting the other side.

Remove the broiler pan from the heat. Put the bacon on the lightly toasted side of the bread, top with the tomato slices and basil, then season to taste. Return the broiler pan to the heat and cook for a further 2 minutes. Serve immediately.

variation: For a more substantial snack, rub the bread with a halved garlic clove before toasting. Cut the garlic clove into thin slivers and insert into the tomato slices, then broil. Put the tomatoes on top of the bread, sprinkle with some Parmesan cheese shavings, and serve with salad greens.

If you're a fan of baked beans, you should really try making your own—you'll be thrilled with the result. Traditionally, dried beans would have been used in this dish (often called Boston baked beans) but using canned reduces the cooking time by two-thirds.

homemade baked beans

1 small ham hock

3 cups canned borlotti or Great Northern beans, drained and rinsed

1 garlic clove, peeled and crushed

1 onion, finely chopped

2 cups vegetable stock

1¼ cup tomato purée or passata

2 tablespoons molasses or black treacle

2 tablespoons tomato paste

1 tablespoon dark brown sugar

1 tablespoon Dijon mustard

1 tablespoon red wine vinegar

freshly ground black pepper

freshly made toast, to serve

a large, flameproof casserole dish

serves 6

Soak the ham hock overnight in cold water (keep it refrigerated).

The next day, preheat the oven to 325°F.

Drain the gammon, wash and pat dry with paper towels. Put into a large, flameproof casserole dish.

Add the beans and all the remaining ingredients to the casserole. Cover and bring slowly to a boil on top of the stove, then transfer to the preheated oven and bake for 1½ hours. Remove the lid and cook for a further 30–45 minutes, until the sauce is syrupy.

Remove the ham hock to a cutting board and slice the meat. Put the toast onto serving plates, top with the beans and gammon and serve hot.

These noodles are not long and thin as one might think, but rather little fried squares of potato and semolina, served either savory or sweet. This sweet cherry compote is based on an original German recipe.

potato noodles
with red cherry compote

1 lb. potatoes, unpeeled

2¾ cups milk

6 tablespoons fine semolina

2 eggs, beaten

6 tablespoons superfine sugar

½ teaspoon ground cinnamon

6 tablespoons butter

sour cream, to serve

½ cup slivered almonds, toasted, to scatter

red cherry compote

1 lb. sweet red cherries, pitted

2 tablespoons superfine sugar

1 strip of orange zest

freshly squeezed juice of 1 orange

2 tablespoons Kirsch

a 9 x 13-inch jelly roll pan, lightly greased

serves 4

Put the potatoes in a saucepan, cover with cold water, bring to a boil, then simmer for 25–30 minutes until tender. When cool enough to handle, peel and pass through a potato ricer into a clean saucepan.

Put the saucepan on the heat and gradually beat in the milk until smooth. Cook, beating continuously (do not allow to catch or burn) until it starts to boil. Sprinkle in the semolina in a thin stream, beating all the time. Continue cooking until the mixture thickens. Remove from the heat and beat in the eggs. Spread onto the prepared jelly roll pan, smoothing the surface. Leave to cool completely.

Turn the mixture out onto a work surface and cut into 1-inch strips. Cut across again into small squares or diamonds.

To make the red cherry compote, put the cherries in a saucepan with the sugar, orange zest, and juice. Stir well, bring to a boil, reduce the heat, cover and simmer for 5–10 minutes or until the cherries are tender. Remove from the heat and stir in the Kirsch. Set aside.

Put the sugar and cinnamon in a saucepan, heat well and stir, then transfer to a large plate or tray.

Melt the butter in a large skillet and cook the potato squares until lightly golden on both sides. Drain well on paper towels then transfer them to the tray of cinnamon sugar and toss well to coat, shaking off any excess.

Serve with sour cream and warm compote, scattered with toasted almonds.

You can't mess about with a classic like this because the old way is still the best. All you need is warm, moist bagels toasted until just crisp, then slathered with creamy cheese, layers of smoked salmon, and a good squeeze of lemon juice.

toasted bagels
with cream cheese & smoked salmon

2 bagels

½ cup cream cheese

4 oz. smoked salmon slices

lemon wedges, for squeezing

freshly ground black pepper

serves 2

Split the bagels in half horizontally and toast on both sides in a toaster, under the broiler or using a stove-top grill pan.

Spread the bottom half of each bagel with cream cheese and fold the slices of smoked salmon on top. Squeeze over plenty of lemon juice, sprinkle with black pepper, and serve topped with the second half of the bagel.

"Welsh rabbit"—also known as "rarebit"—is a glorified version of cheese on toast. It dates back to mid-sixteenth century England and has evolved into countless variations. This easy-to-make rarebit is hard to beat as a comforting snack or light brunch.

rarebit

1½ tablespoons butter

4 shallots or 1 onion, sliced

1 cup grated Cheddar or Gruyère cheese, grated

⅓ cup ale or lager

1 teaspoon mustard

a pinch of sea salt

2 eggs, lightly beaten

4 slices of bread

freshly ground black pepper

serves 2–4

Melt the butter in a heavy-bottomed saucepan, add the shallots and cook until softened. Add the cheese, ale, mustard, and salt. Stir over low heat until the cheese has melted.

Add the beaten eggs and stir until the mixture has thickened slightly, about 2–3 minutes. Don't overcook it or you will end up with scrambled eggs.

Meanwhile, toast the bread on both sides, then spoon the cheese mixture onto the toast and cook under a hot broiler until puffed and gold-flecked. Serve with lots of black pepper.

We all get the munchies, especially if we've missed breakfast. Instead of reaching for that packet of potato chips or candy bar, make one of these snacks for brunch. Pure, fresh, and nutritious food, they will stop all rumblings in your tummy and taste good too.

zucchini & cheddar
on toast

2 zucchini, grated

1⅔ cups mature cheddar or Monterey Jack cheese, grated

1 shallot, finely chopped

1 small egg

a dash of Worcestershire sauce

4 slices of bread, toasted

sea salt and freshly ground black pepper

serves 4

Preheat the broiler. Put the grated zucchini in a clean, dry kitchen towel and twist tightly, squeezing out all the excess liquid.

Transfer to a mixing bowl and add the cheese, shallot, egg, Worcestershire sauce, salt, and pepper. Stir thoroughly.

Put the toasted bread onto a baking sheet, pile the zucchini mixture on top and cook under a medium-hot broiler until golden brown. Serve whilst still hot.

This Italian-inspired toasted sandwich is extremely versatile and makes a delicious and quick brunch or lunch dish. It takes only minutes to prepare and will keep you satisfied until dinner time.

sardine bruschetta

4 oz. canned sardines

1 teaspoon balsamic vinegar

1 slice of whole-wheat bread, lightly toasted

1 tablespoon finely grated cheddar cheese (optional)

3–4 cherry tomatoes, halved

serves 1

Preheat the broiler. Put the sardines and vinegar in a bowl and mash with a fork. Pile the sardines on top of the toasted bread and sprinkle with the grated cheese, if using.

Transfer to a broiler pan with the tomatoes and cook under a preheated broiler for 2–3 minutes, or until the cheese is golden brown and the tomatoes are hot.

Put the tomatoes on top of the toast and cut it into fingers.

Fish cakes of any kind make a perfect brunch, but these, made with salmon and sweet potatoes, are particularly good. Keep any leftover lemon and rosemary mayonnaise in the fridge for up to 3 days.

salmon & sweet potato fish cakes

1 lb. salmon fillets

1 tablespoon olive oil

1 lb. sweet potatoes, peeled and cubed

4 scallions, finely chopped

1 small garlic clove, peeled and crushed

grated zest and juice of ½ lemon

⅓ cup fine cornmeal

sunflower oil, for frying

sea salt and freshly ground black pepper

salad greens, to serve

lemon and rosemary mayonnaise

leaves from 1 sprig of fresh rosemary

½ teaspoon sea salt

2 egg yolks

1 teaspoon Dijon mustard

1¼ cups olive oil

1–2 tablespoons freshly squeezed lemon juice

serves 4

Preheat the oven to 400°F.

Put the salmon fillets on a sheet of aluminum foil and drizzle with the olive oil. Wrap the foil loosely around the salmon and bake for 20–25 minutes. Remove from the oven and leave until cold. Flake the flesh with a fork, reserving any juices from the package.

Meanwhile, cook the potatoes in lightly salted, boiling water for 15 minutes. Drain well, return to the saucepan, and dry out briefly over low heat. Mash coarsely and set aside to cool.

Add the fish with the juices, scallions, garlic, lemon zest, and juice to the cooled potatoes. Season to taste and mix well. Shape into 8 small fish cakes and refrigerate for 30 minutes.

To make the lemon and rosemary mayonnaise, grind the rosemary leaves and salt to a powder with a mortar and pestle. Put in a food processor with the egg yolks and mustard and blend briefly. With the motor running, gradually add the oil through the funnel until thickened and glossy. Add lemon juice to taste.

Coat the fish cakes with cornmeal. Put enough oil to cover the base in a skillet and heat until hot. Add the fish cakes and fry for 4–5 minutes on each side until golden. Serve with the mayonnaise and salad greens.

This is such a classic sandwich and deservedly so, since it is really very delicious! Always use very fresh bread—all the better for soaking up those juices—and for this particular sandwich, unbleached bread is best.

steak & tomato sandwich

olive oil, for greasing

4 sirloin steaks, about 3½ oz. each

8 slices of bread

butter, for spreading

4 teaspoons Dijon mustard

2 large, ripe tomatoes, sliced

a handful of arugula, about 4 oz.

sea salt and freshly ground black pepper

serves 4

Heat a stove-top grill pan or a nonstick skillet with a little olive oil. When very hot, add the steaks and cook to taste: 1 minute on each side for rare steak, 2 minutes each side for medium, or 3 minutes each side for well done.

Meanwhile, spread 4 slices of the bread with butter and mustard, then add the sliced tomatoes and arugula.

Top with the cooked steak and sprinkle with seasoning. Butter the remaining slices of bread and put them on top of the steaks. Press together, wrap in a napkin to catch those drips, and eat.

Indian salads or raitas almost always include yogurt as the main element of the dressing, with toasted spices as the flavor note. Use almost any crisp fruit or vegetable in this salad—vary according to what's in season.

fruit & vegetables
with yogurt dressing

¼ cup cashews

4 small crisp lettuces, cut into wedges or torn into pieces

6 segments pomelo or grapefruit (preferably pink), membranes removed, segments pulled into 2–3 pieces (optional)

12 large red or white grapes, or both, halved lengthwise and seeded

6 red radishes, finely sliced

1 mini cucumber, halved lengthwise, seeded and thinly sliced

1-inch piece fresh ginger, peeled and thinly sliced

¼ cup unsweetened flaked coconut, soaked in water if dried (optional)

sprigs of cilantro (optional)

yogurt dressing

a pinch of lovage seeds (optional)

1 teaspoon mustard seeds

a pinch of hot red pepper flakes

½ teaspoon salt

½ teaspoon sugar

1-inch piece fresh ginger, peeled

1 cup plain yogurt

serves 4

To make the yogurt dressing, put the lovage and mustard seeds and the red pepper flakes in a dry skillet and toast over medium heat until aromatic. Transfer to a small bowl and leave to cool. Add the salt and sugar, then grate the ginger and squeeze the gratings into the bowl. Stir in the yogurt.

Put the cashews in the same pan and toast over medium heat until golden. Do not allow to burn. Remove from the heat, transfer to a small bowl and leave to cool. When cool, chop coarsely with a knife.

Put the lettuce wedges onto a plate, add the pomelo pieces, if using, grapes, radishes, cucumber, and ginger. Spoon over the dressing sparingly. Sprinkle with the cashews, coconut, and cilantro, if using.

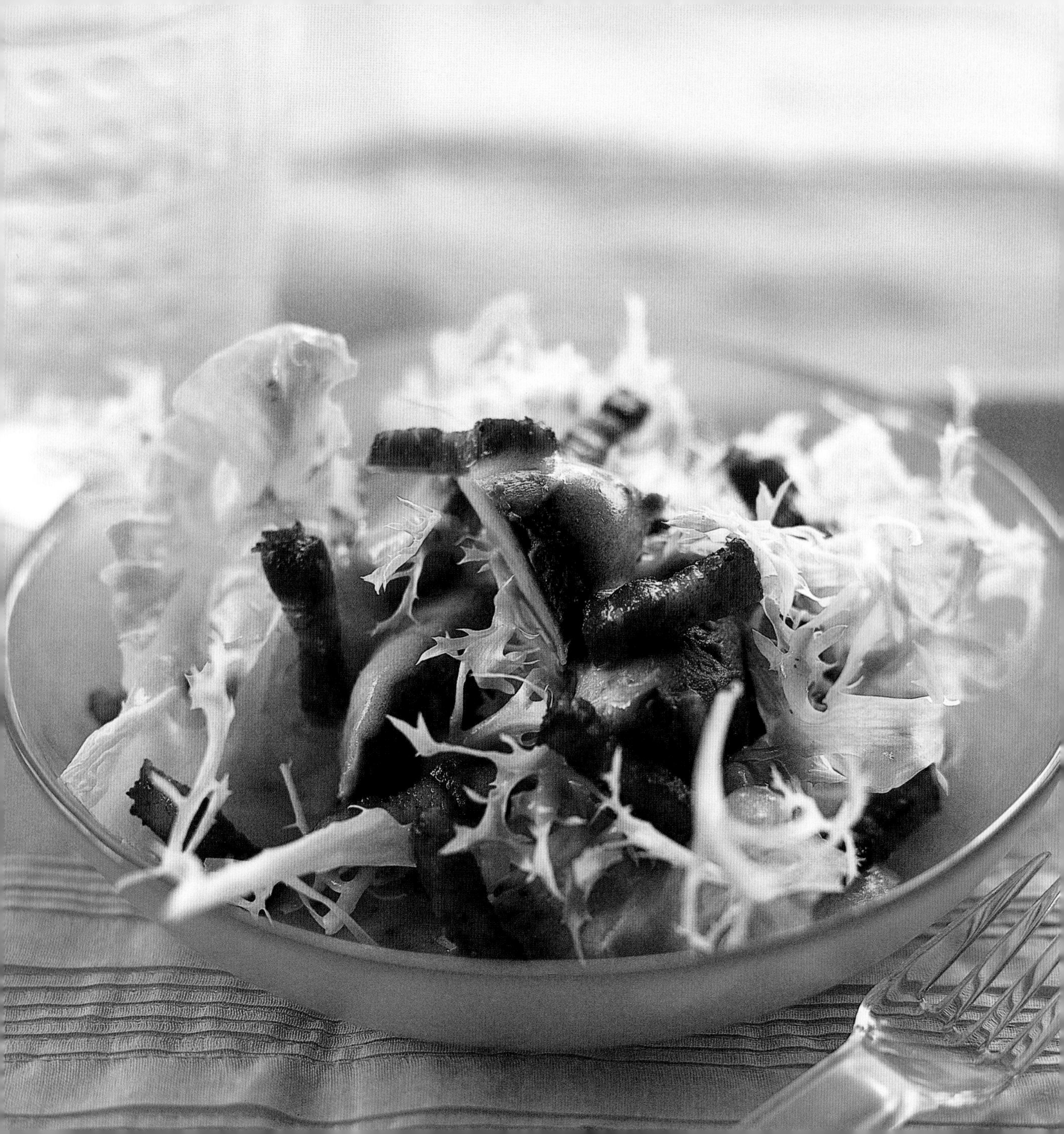

Avocado is so creamy and delicious it can really be used as a dressing in itself. Avocado loves salty things, like seafood, smoked food, and bacon. Share it for brunch with salad leaves, smoked bacon, and a regular dressing.

avocado salad

6 very thin slices smoked bacon or prosciutto, or 7 oz. cubed pancetta

1 tablespoon olive oil

8 oz. salad greens (a mixture of soft, crisp, and peppery)

1–2 ripe avocados

dressing

6 tablespoons extra virgin olive oil

1 tablespoon cider vinegar or rice vinegar

1 garlic clove, peeled and crushed

1 teaspoon Dijon mustard

sea salt and freshly ground black pepper

serves 4

Cut the bacon into 3–4 pieces. Heat a skillet, brush with the olive oil, add the bacon and cook over medium heat, without disturbing, until crisp on one side. Using tongs, turn the pieces over and sauté until crisp and papery but not too brown. Remove and drain on paper towels.

To make the dressing, put all the ingredients in a salad bowl and beat with a fork or small whisk. When ready to serve, add the salad greens and turn in the dressing, using your hands. Cut the avocados in half and remove the stones. Using a teaspoon, scoop out balls of avocado into the salad. Toss gently if you like (though this will send the avocado to the bottom of the bowl.) Add the bacon and serve.

easy eggs

Perfect for a leisurely breakfast or brunch. Adding a drizzle of honey and a pinch of cinnamon to the tomatoes gives them an irresistibly warm, scented sweetness that goes perfectly with the smooth, creamy eggs and earthy, pungent rye.

creamy scrambled eggs on rye
with cinnamon-honey roasted tomatoes

3 plum tomatoes

¼ teaspoon ground cinnamon

1 teaspoon clear honey

½ tablespoon olive oil

4 large eggs

1 tablespoon heavy cream

4 slices of light rye bread

2 tablespoons butter, plus extra for spreading

sea salt and freshly ground black pepper

serves 2

Preheat the oven to 425°F.

Cut the tomatoes in half lengthwise and arrange in a baking dish, cut side up. Sprinkle with cinnamon, salt, and pepper and drizzle over the honey and olive oil. Roast in the preheated oven for 30 minutes, pouring any juices back over the tomatoes part way through cooking.

When the tomatoes are nearly cooked, put the eggs and cream in a bowl, season and beat briefly. Toast the rye bread in a toaster or under the broiler and keep it warm.

Melt the butter in a small, nonstick saucepan over medium-low heat until sizzling. Pour in the eggs and cook gently for 1–2 minutes, stirring constantly, until thick and creamy. (The eggs will continue to cook after you remove the pan from the heat, so be careful not to overcook.)

Quickly butter the rye toast and put 2 slices on each plate. Spoon the scrambled eggs on top and pile 3 tomato halves on each portion. Spoon over any extra tomato juices, sprinkle with pepper, and serve immediately.

note: Don't use dark, moist rye bread such as pumpernickel for this recipe. It doesn't toast well, and won't give the delicious crispness of a light rye.

Stirring a little creamy goat cheese into lightly scrambled eggs transforms a simple dish into a delicious and rather special brunch. The nasturtium flowers are optional, but they do add a delightful flash of color as well as a delicate peppery flavor.

creamy eggs
with goat cheese

12 eggs

½ cup light cream

2 tablespoons chopped fresh marjoram

4 tablespoons butter

6 oz. firm goat cheese, diced

a handful of nasturtium flowers, torn (optional)

sea salt and freshly ground black pepper

toasted walnut bread, to serve

serves 4

Beat the eggs in a bowl with the cream, marjoram and a little seasoning. Melt the butter in a nonstick saucepan, add the eggs and stir over low heat until they are beginning to set.

Stir in the goat cheese and continue to cook briefly, still stirring, until the cheese melts into the eggs. Add the nasturtium flowers, if using, and spoon onto the toast. Serve immediately.

Prosciutto, sautéed so it becomes really crisp, adds a lovely texture to the creamy sauce and egg yolks. Try substituting smoked salmon for the ham or, for a vegetarian version, replace the ham with wilted spinach as in the Eggs Florentine on page 121.

eggs benedict
on toasted muffins

4 large slices of prosciutto

4 eggs

1 tablespoon vinegar
(preferably distilled)

4 English muffins

hollandaise sauce

2 sticks unsalted butter

3 egg yolks

1 teaspoon freshly squeezed
lemon juice

sea salt and freshly ground
black pepper

serves 4

To make the hollandaise sauce, put the butter in a small saucepan and melt it gently over very low heat, without letting it brown. Put the egg yolks, 2 tablespoons water, and lemon juice in a blender and process until frothy. With the blade turning, gradually pour in the melted butter in a steady stream until the sauce is thickened and glossy. Transfer the sauce to a bowl set over a saucepan of hot water. Cover and keep the sauce warm.

Broil or sauté the slices of prosciutto until really crisp and keep them warm in a low oven. To poach the eggs, bring a saucepan of lightly salted water to a boil. Add the vinegar and reduce to a gentle simmer. Swirl the water well with a fork and crack 2 eggs into the water. Cook for 3 minutes, remove with a slotted spoon and repeat with the remaining 2 eggs.

Meanwhile, toast the muffins whole and top each with a slice of crisp prosciutto. Put the poached eggs on top of the ham. Spoon over the hollandaise, sprinkle with seasoning, and serve at once.

If you haven't the time to make your own, you can buy excellent ready-made hollandaise sauce in stores, taking all the hassle out of making this divine breakfast. A good-quality cheese sauce works just as well.

eggs florentine
on toasted muffins

2 eggs

1 tablespoon vinegar (preferably distilled)

1 tablespoon butter, plus extra to spread

8 oz. baby spinach leaves

a pinch of freshly grated nutmeg

2 English muffins

2–4 tablespoons Hollandaise Sauce (page 118)

sea salt and freshly ground black pepper

serves 2

To poach the eggs, bring a saucepan of lightly salted water to a boil. Add the vinegar and reduce to a gentle simmer. Swirl the water well with a fork and crack the eggs into the water. Cook for 3 minutes and remove with a slotted spoon.

Meanwhile, melt the butter in a saucepan, then add the spinach. Cook for about 3 minutes, stirring occasionally, until the spinach begins to wilt. Season with nutmeg and salt and pepper. Remove from the heat, cover and keep it warm.

Toast the muffins whole and spread with butter. Spoon some spinach onto each muffin (taking care to drain off any excess liquid as you do so.) Set an egg on top, spoon over the hollandaise sauce, sprinkle with a little more pepper and serve immediately.

Smoked salmon and eggs is one of those combinations that works at any time of day. This is an easy, elegant dish that takes no time at all and makes the perfect breakfast treat. Surprise someone special with this breakfast in bed.

baked eggs
with smoked salmon & chives

8 oz. smoked salmon slices, chopped

1 tablespoon snipped fresh chives

4 eggs

¼ cup heavy cream

freshly ground black pepper

freshly made toast, to serve

4 shallow ovenproof dishes or ramekins, well buttered

serves 4

Preheat the oven to 350°F.

Divide the smoked salmon and chives between the 4 dishes. Make a small indent in the salmon with the back of a spoon and break an egg into the hollow. Sprinkle with a little pepper and spoon the cream over the top.

Put the ramekins in a roasting pan and half-fill the pan with boiling water. Bake for about 10–15 minutes, or until the eggs have just set. Remove from the oven, let cool for a few minutes, then serve with toast.

When time is short, but something warm and comforting is nevertheless required, these baked eggs go down a treat. The spinach adds both color and a healthy mineral kick. Very little effort is required but the results are delicious.

eggs cocotte

2 oz. fresh spinach, chopped

4 eggs

4 tablespoons milk

¾ cup grated Parmesan cheese

sea salt and freshly ground
black pepper

4 ovenproof ramekins, buttered

serves 4

Preheat the oven to 400°F.

Divide the spinach between the prepared ramekins. Crack an egg on top, add a spoonful of milk to each, then season and top with the Parmesan. Put the ramekins on a baking sheet in the preheated oven and cook for 6 minutes.

Tea-smoked salmon replaces the more traditional smoked haddock in this version of the classic Anglo-Indian breakfast dish. It is a substantial meal, perfect for when you've got a big day ahead of you.

kedgeree
with tea-smoked salmon

3 tablespoons butter

1 onion, finely chopped

1¼ cups basmati rice

1 tablespoon curry paste

4 cardamom pods, crushed

1 cinnamon stick, crushed

1 teaspoon ground turmeric

2¼ cups fish or vegetable stock

2 hard-cooked eggs, peeled and quartered

chopped fresh chives and parsley, to serve (optional)

sea salt and freshly ground black pepper

tea-smoked salmon

1 lb. salmon fillet

½ cup rice

½ cup tea leaves

½ cup brown sugar

serves 6

Melt the butter in a saucepan, add the onion, and sauté for 5 minutes. Add the rice, curry paste, and spices, stir once, then add the stock. Bring to a boil, cover, and simmer over very low heat for 20 minutes.

Meanwhile, to smoke the salmon, cut the fillet into 4 equal pieces and sprinkle with seasoning. Line a wok with a sheet of foil and put the rice, tea leaves and sugar in the bottom. Arrange a rack over the top. Cover and heat for 5–8 minutes, until the mixture starts smoking. Slide the fish fillets, skin-side down, onto the rack, cover, and smoke over high heat for 4 minutes. Remove the wok from the heat but leave undisturbed for a further 3 minutes. Remove the fish and keep it warm.

Skin and flake the salmon into large pieces and add to the spiced rice. Add salt and pepper to taste and mix briefly with a fork. Cover and leave for 5 minutes. Serve topped with the egg quarters and sprinkled with the chopped herbs.

This creamy, light topping is packed with the flavor of asparagus. For the best results, make this with the freshest asparagus. If you have some, you can drizzle a little truffle oil over for a special occasion, as the flavors of eggs and truffle go very well together.

egg, mascarpone, & asparagus
crostini

1 thin French baguette, sliced into thin rounds

extra virgin olive oil, for brushing

½ cup unsalted butter, softened

¼ cup chopped fresh parsley

4 scallions, finely chopped

12 spears of fresh green asparagus, stems trimmed

6 large eggs

¼–⅓ cup mascarpone cheese, softened

truffle oil, for drizzling (optional)

sea salt and freshly ground black pepper

serves 6

Preheat the oven to 375°F.

To make the crostini, brush both sides of each slice of bread with olive oil and spread out on a baking sheet. Bake for about 10 minutes until crisp and golden.

Meanwhile, beat the butter with the parsley and scallions, and season to taste with salt and black pepper.

Cook the asparagus in boiling salted water for about 6 minutes until tender. Cut off and reserve the tips, and slice the stems.

Boil the eggs for 6–8 minutes. Plunge into cold water for a couple of minutes, then shell and coarsely mash with a fork. Add the scallion mixture and mascarpone and stir until creamy. Fold in the sliced asparagus stems, then season with salt and pepper.

Spread the egg mixture thickly onto the crostini, top with the asparagus tips, and sprinkle with a couple of drops of truffle oil, if using, or some extra virgin olive oil.

Even as an adult you never tire of dunking toast into the perfect soft-cooked egg. It's even better when you dip in asparagus spears. Remember the eggs need to be at room temperature before they are plunged into boiling water.

soft-cooked eggs
with asparagus soldiers

24 thick asparagus spears

8 large eggs, at room temperature

sea salt and freshly ground black pepper

freshly made toast, to serve

serves 4

Tie the asparagus into bunches of 6 stems with kitchen twine. Steam or boil them for 3–4 minutes, or until just tender. Drain and keep them warm.

Meanwhile, cook the eggs in gently boiling water for 4 minutes, then transfer them to eggcups. Remove the tops of the eggs with a spoon and season to taste with salt and black pepper. Serve with toast and cooked asparagus for dunking.

Ever since this Mexican dish began cropping up in south-western diners, huevos rancheros has become as mainstream as omelets on menus across the country. You can use store-bought salsa for this, but be sure to use the cooked variety instead of raw.

huevos rancheros

4 corn tortillas

3 tablespoons vegetable oil

1 cup grated mild cheese, such as cheddar or Monterey Jack

4 eggs

sea salt and freshly ground pepper

salsa

6 plum tomatoes, halved

2 jalapeño peppers

8 garlic cloves, unpeeled

¼ cup chopped cilantro

1 teaspoon Tabasco Sauce or favorite hot sauce

1 small red onion, finely chopped, to serve

serves 4

To make the salsa, place the halved tomatoes cut-side up in a shallow roasting pan. Season and place on the top rack under a preheated broiler. Broil for about 10 minutes, or until charred.

Preheat the oven to 400°F.

Meanwhile, in a dry, nonstick skillet, blacken the peppers and garlic cloves. Keep turning to color all sides. When done, peel the garlic and place in a food processor. Put the peppers in a plastic bag, tie a knot in the bag and leave the peppers to steam for a few minutes, then peel, seed and stem. Add the flesh to the food processor along with the tomatoes, 2 tablespoons of the cilantro and the Tabasco. Season and pulse until smooth. Pour into a saucepan and cook briefly over medium heat to warm through.

Brush the tortillas with 2 tablespoons of the oil and bake for 5 minutes until golden. Divide the cheese between the tortillas and return to the oven for 5 minutes until the cheese has melted. Turn off the oven, open the door and leave the tortillas in to keep warm. Fry the eggs in a nonstick skillet in the remaining tablespoon of oil. Place the tortillas on 4 plates and slip an egg on top of each. Spoon the warm salsa over each and sprinkle with the chopped onion and remaining cilantro.

This classic tortilla consists of just three ingredients: eggs, potatoes, and onions. Together, they are transformed into an unbelievably delicious dish. Tortillas may be cut into squares or wedges or even between chunks of bread—a favorite way of eating them in Spain.

classic spanish tortilla

1 large onion

3–4 tablespoons extra virgin olive or sunflower oil

4 potatoes, about 1 lb., peeled

5 extra-large eggs

sea salt and freshly ground black pepper

an 8-inch heavy, nonstick skillet (measure the base, not the top)

serves 2–3

Cut the onion in half, then slice thinly lengthwise and separate into slivers. Heat 3 tablespoons of the oil in the skillet.

Thinly slice the potatoes, then add them to the skillet in layers, alternating with the onion. Cook for 10–15 minutes over medium-low heat, lifting and turning occasionally, until just tender. The potatoes and onions should not brown very much.

Meanwhile, break the eggs into a large bowl, beat lightly with a fork, and season with salt and pepper. Remove the potatoes and onions from the skillet and drain, reserving any oil. Add them to the bowl of eggs and mix gently.

Heat the reserved oil in the skillet, adding a little extra if necessary. Add the potato and egg mixture, spreading it evenly in the pan. Cook over medium-low heat until the bottom is golden brown and the top almost set.

Put a plate or flat saucepan lid on top of the skillet and invert the pan so the tortilla drops onto the plate or lid. Return to the pan, brown-side up, and cook on top of the stove for 2–3 minutes until the other side is lightly browned. Turn again and transfer to a serving plate, with the most attractive side upward. Serve hot or at room temperature, cut into wedges.

This is a great way to cook an omelet—once prepared, it can finish cooking in the oven, making the whole thing quite relaxed. It is ideal for a late, lazy breakfast, but good enough to eat at any time of the day. Make sure the pan handle is ovenproof.

baked brunch omelet

2 tablespoons sunflower oil

4 slices of smoked bacon,
cut into strips

1 onion, finely sliced

1 medium potato, cubed

½ cups sliced, white mushrooms

5 extra-large eggs

½ cup milk

¾ cup grated sharp cheddar cheese

1 tablespoon unsalted butter

1 tablespoon freshly grated
Parmesan cheese

sea salt and freshly ground
black pepper

*an 8-inch heavy, nonstick skillet
(measure the base, not the top)*

serves 2–3

Preheat the oven to 400°F.

Heat the sunflower oil in the skillet, add the bacon, onion, and potato and sauté for 6 minutes, or until the potatoes start to brown. Add the mushrooms and sauté for 2 minutes.

Meanwhile, put the eggs and milk in a large bowl and beat lightly with a fork, just enough to mix the yolks and whites. Season with salt and plenty of pepper. Stir in three-fourths of the cheddar.

Using a slotted spoon, transfer the potato mixture to the bowl of eggs and mix well. Add the butter to the skillet and, when it starts to foam, pour in the omelet mixture. Sprinkle with the remaining cheese and transfer to the preheated oven.

Cook for 12–15 minutes, or until just set. Loosen the edges with a spatula and slide onto a warmed serving plate. Sprinkle with Parmesan, cut into wedges, and serve immediately.

Loaded with sausages, fried potatoes, and onions, this dish is perfect comfort food. Ring the changes with different kinds of sausage—try slices of chorizo, spicy Italian sausages, or even frankfurters.

sausage, potato, & onion tortilla

3–4 tablespoons extra virgin olive or sunflower oil

6 pork chipolata sausages with herbs

1 onion

3 potatoes, about 12 oz. thinly sliced

5 extra-large eggs

sea salt and freshly ground black pepper

a 9-inch heavy, nonstick skillet (measure the base, not the top)

serves 2–3

Heat 1 tablespoon of the oil in the skillet. Add the sausages and sauté for 8–10 minutes, turning them frequently. Remove and set aside. Wipe out the skillet with paper towels.

Cut the onion in half and then into slivers lengthwise.

Heat 2 tablespoons of the oil in the cleaned skillet. Add the potatoes, layering them with the onions. Cook for 10–15 minutes over medium-low heat, lifting and turning occasionally, until just tender. The potatoes and onions should not brown very much.

Meanwhile, break the eggs into a large bowl, add salt and pepper and beat briefly with a fork. Remove the potatoes and onions from the skillet with a slotted spoon and add to the egg mixture. Thickly slice the sausages and mix with the eggs and potatoes.

Return the skillet to the heat, adding a little more oil if necessary. Add the potato and egg mixture spreading it evenly. Cook over medium-low heat until the bottom is golden brown and the top has almost set.

Put a plate or flat saucepan lid on top of the skillet, then invert so the tortilla drops onto the plate or lid. Slide back into the skillet, brown-side up, and cook for 2–3 minutes until lightly browned underneath. Serve hot or warm, cut into wedges.

Baby spinach is essential for this recipe because the leaves wilt and soften quickly, so you needn't remove the stalks or chop the leaves. Pancetta (smoked Italian bacon), adds a special depth of flavor. Like all frittatas, any leftover makes a good bag lunch.

spinach & pancetta frittata

6 extra-large eggs

1 tablespoon extra virgin olive or sunflower oil

4 oz. pancetta cubes or smoked bacon, but into strips

4 scallions, chopped

1 garlic clove, peeled and finely chopped

1½ cups baby spinach

sea salt and freshly ground black pepper

a 12–inch heavy skillet (measure the base, not the top)

serves 4

Break the eggs into a bowl and beat briefly with a fork. Season well.

Heat 1 tablespoon of the oil in the skillet. Add the pancetta and cook over medium heat for 3–4 minutes until they start to brown.

Add the scallions, garlic, and spinach and stir-fry for 3–4 minutes or until the spinach has wilted and the onions have softened.

Pour the egg mixture into the skillet, quickly mix into the other ingredients, and stop stirring. Reduce to a low heat and cook for 8–10 minutes, or until the top has almost set. Slide under a preheated broiler to finish cooking the top. Serve hot or cold, cut into wedges.

Porcini are difficult to buy fresh, but are widely available dried. They are one of the best mushrooms, with an intense, rich flavor that will pervade the omelet. Strain their soaking liquid and add a spoonful to the omelet mixture, or keep it for a soup or stew.

porcini frittata

½ oz. dried porcini mushrooms

6 large eggs

3 tablespoons mascarpone cheese

3 tablespoons chopped
fresh flat-leaf parsley

3 tablespoons extra virgin olive
or sunflower oil

1 onion, halved and sliced

2½ cups sliced white button
mushrooms

1 tablespoon freshly grated
Parmesan cheese

1 tablespoon unsalted butter

3 oz. fresh wild mushrooms

sea salt and freshly ground
black pepper

*an 8-inch heavy, nonstick skillet
(measure the base, not the top)*

serves 2–3

Put the porcini in a small bowl and cover with warm water. Let soak for 30 minutes. Break 1 of the eggs into a bowl, add the mascarpone, and mix well. Add the remaining eggs and beat lightly with a fork. Stir in the parsley and season.

Heat 1 tablespoon of the oil in the skillet, add the onion and cook over low heat until soft. Add another tablespoon of oil and the white mushrooms and cook for 5 minutes. Drain the porcini (reserving the soaking liquid) and chop if large. Add to the pan and cook for 2 minutes.

Using a slotted spoon, transfer the mushrooms and onions to the eggs and mix gently.

Wipe out the skillet with paper towels, add the remaining oil, and heat gently. Add the frittata mixture and cook over low heat until browned on the underside and nearly set on top. Sprinkle with Parmesan and slide under a preheated broiler to finish cooking the top and melt the cheese. Transfer to a warm serving plate.

Melt the butter in the skillet, add the wild mushrooms, and sauté quickly. Spoon over the top of the frittata and serve.

It is important to start folding the omelet while it is still slightly liquid in the center to avoid it overcooking and becoming tough and leathery. Make sure the person who is going to eat it is ready first, rather than the omelet.

smoked salmon omelet

3 oz. smoked salmon, cut into thin strips

1 tablespoon milk

3 extra-large eggs

2 teaspoons unsalted butter

2 tablespoons sour cream or crème fraîche

1 tablespoon chopped fresh dill

sea salt and freshly ground black pepper

a 7-inch heavy omelet pan (measure the base, not the top)

serves 1

Put half the smoked salmon in a bowl, add the milk, and let stand for 15 minutes.

Break the eggs into a bowl and beat lightly with a fork. Season with salt and pepper, then stir in the milk and smoked salmon.

Heat the butter in the omelet pan. When the butter starts to foam, pour in the egg mixture and cook over medium-high heat, drawing the mixture from the sides to the center as it sets. Let the liquid flow and fill the space at the sides.

After a short time, the omelet will be cooked but still creamy in the center. Top the omelet with the sour cream or crème fraîche and sprinkle with chopped dill and the remaining smoked salmon.

Fold over one-third of the omelet to the center, then fold over the remaining third, slide onto a warmed plate, and serve immediately.

An ideal tasty brunch dish, especially for al fresco dining served with a crisp salad, this omelet is just bursting with Mediterranean flavors. It is worth buying tomatoes ripened on the vine for their extra taste explosion.

feta cheese & tomato
open omelet

5 extra-large eggs

2 tablespoons chopped fresh basil

1 tablespoon chopped fresh mint

3 scallions, finely chopped

2 tablespoons sunflower oil

3 oz. feta cheese, crumbled

8 small cherry tomatoes, halved

sea salt and freshly ground black pepper

a 7-inch heavy omelet pan (measure the base not the top)

serves 2

Break the eggs into a bowl and beat lightly with a fork. Season with salt and pepper, add 2 tablespoons water, the basil, mint, and scallions and mix briefly.

Heat the oil in the omelet pan. Pour in the egg mixture and cook over medium heat for 4–5 minutes, drawing the mixture from the sides to the center until the omelet is half cooked.

Top with the feta and the tomato halves, cut-side up, and cook for 2 minutes. Slide under a preheated broiler and cook until light golden brown. Slide onto a warmed plate and serve immediately.

A fusion of tortilla-inspired wraps with Portuguese-style piri-piri chicken which make an even more filling alternative to standard omelets. Increase or reduce the amount of piri-piri sauce in the marinade depending on how hot you would like it.

omelet wraps

2 tablespoons extra virgin olive oil

freshly squeezed juice of 1 lime

2 tablespoons chopped cilantro

1 tablespoon piri-piri sauce, or 2–3 dashes of Tabasco

2 large, skinless chicken breasts, cut into thin strips

5 large eggs

2 tablespoons milk

2 tablespoons snipped fresh chives

1 avocado, halved, pitted, peeled, and chopped

6 cherry tomatoes, quartered

4 teaspoons unsalted butter

sea salt and freshly ground black pepper

a 7-inch heavy omelet pan (measure the base not the top)

serves 2

Put the olive oil, lime juice, and cilantro in a bowl and mix with a fork. Put half the mixture in a shallow dish, add the piri-piri sauce and mix well. Add the chicken and stir to coat with the marinade. Set aside for 30 minutes.

Break the eggs into a bowl, then add the milk and season with salt and pepper. Beat lightly with a fork. Mix in the chives. Add the avocado, cherry tomatoes, the remaining olive oil, and lime juice and stir gently to coat.

Stir-fry the chicken in a nonstick skillet for 3–4 minutes, or until the juices run clear, then remove from the heat and set aside.

Meanwhile melt half the butter in the omelet pan over medium-high heat and swirl it around to coat the bottom and sides of the pan. When the butter starts to foam, pour in half the eggs.

Tip the pan to spread the eggs evenly over the base, leave for about 5 seconds, then draw the edges of the eggs to the center, letting the liquid egg flow to the sides. When the omelet has just set, transfer to a warm plate, add the remaining butter to the pan, and cook the second omelet in the same way.

Mix the cooked chicken with the avocado and tomatoes and divide between the two omelets, spooning the mixture in a line down the middle. Roll up the omelets, cut in half, and serve.

fresh from the oven

This recipe is inspired by the little custard tarts (*pasteis de nata*) found all over Portugal. These divine little tarts make an ideal sweet treat for midmorning, served with a shot of the strong but fragrant cardamom coffee.

baby custard tarts
with cardamom coffee

10 oz. ready-made sweet pastry dough, thawed if frozen

1¼ cups milk

⅓ cup superfine sugar

1 teaspoon vanilla extract

2 egg yolks

1 whole egg

½ tablespoon cornstarch

ground cinnamon, to dust

cardamom coffee

3 cardamom pods

4 tablespoons espresso coffee beans

a 3-inch cookie cutter (optional)

2 x 12-cup mini-muffin pan or jam tart trays

baking beans (optional)

makes 24 small tarts

Preheat the oven to 400°F.

Roll out the pastry on a lightly floured surface. Using a cookie cutter or an upturned glass, stamp out 24 rounds about 3 inches across. Press the rounds carefully into the muffin pans, lightly prick the pastry bases, and line each with a circle of baking parchment.

Fill the cases with baking beans (or rice if you don't have baking beans) and bake for 5 minutes. Remove the paper and beans and return to the oven for a few more minutes to crisp. Set aside and reduce the oven temperature to 300°F.

Meanwhile, to make the filling, put the milk, sugar, and vanilla extract in a saucepan and bring to a boil. Simmer until reduced by about half.

Put the egg yolks, whole egg, and cornstarch in a bowl and beat well. Gradually beat in the vanilla milk. Pour the mixture into the tart shells and bake in the preheated oven for 10 minutes, until the surface of the custard is glossy and the centers are just set. Set aside until cold.

To make the coffee, remove the seeds from the cardamom pods and grind with the coffee beans, in a coffee grinder. Use the ground cardamom coffee to make espresso in the normal way.

Dust the tarts with cinnamon and serve with a small cup of the coffee.

Seville orange marmalade—a classic breakfast preserve—makes a delicious main ingredient for these simple muffins. Eat them shortly after they have come out of the oven, when they are still warm—they melt in the mouth.

marmalade muffins

1 cup all-purpose flour

1 cup whole-wheat flour

1 tablespoon baking powder

a large pinch of sea salt

1 large egg, lightly beaten

1¼ cups milk

2 teaspoons freshly squeezed orange juice

¼ cup vegetable oil or melted butter

⅔ cup thick-cut Seville orange marmalade

a deep 12-cup muffin pan, well greased

makes 12 muffins

Preheat the oven to 425°F.

Sift the dry ingredients in a large bowl, mix thoroughly, then make a well in the center. Add the egg, milk, orange juice, and oil. Stir the marmalade to break up any large clumps, then add to the bowl. Mix quickly to form a coarse, slightly streaky batter. Do not beat or overmix or the muffins will be tough and dry. Spoon the mixture into the prepared muffin pan, filling each cup about two-thirds full.

Bake in the preheated oven for 20 minutes, or until lightly browned and firm to the touch. Let cool in the pan for 1 minute, then turn out onto a wire rack. Eat warm. The muffins should be eaten within 24 hours or left to cool, then frozen for up to 1 month.

Everyone loves a blueberry muffin. These are extra special as they are packed with ground almonds and flavored with lemon zest and juice to make them slightly tangy. Use wild berries if you can find them.

lemon, almond, & blueberry muffins

⅓ cup whole blanched almonds

1¾ cups all-purpose flour, sifted

1 tablespoon baking powder, sifted

⅓ cup superfine sugar

grated zest of 1 lemon

1 large egg

1¼ cups milk

2 teaspoons freshly squeezed lemon juice

¼ cup vegetable oil

1 cup fresh or frozen blueberries (if frozen, use them straight from the freezer)

a deep 12-cup muffin pan, well greased

makes 12 muffins

Preheat the oven to 400°F.

Put the almonds in a food processor and grind to a coarse meal. They should have more texture than commercially ground almonds. Transfer to a large bowl and mix with the flour, baking powder, sugar, and lemon zest.

Lightly beat the egg with the milk, lemon juice, and vegetable oil. Add to the dry ingredients and stir just enough to make a coarse, lumpy mixture. Add the blueberries and mix quickly, using as few strokes as possible, leaving the mixture slightly streaky. Do not beat or overmix or the muffins will be tough and dry.

Spoon the mixture into the prepared muffin pan, filling each cup about two-thirds full. Bake in the preheated oven for 20–25 minutes, or until golden and firm to the touch. Let cool in the pan for 1 minute, then turn out onto a wire rack. Eat warm. The muffins should be eaten within 24 hours or left to cool, then frozen for up to 1 month.

Fresh peaches make these muffins special. Serve warm with Greek yogurt. With their fresh fruit, oats, and optional side serving of yogurt, these bakes really are a complete breakfast in a muffin.

fresh peach & oat muffins

1⅓ cups rolled oats

1⅓ cups buttermilk

1 large egg, lightly beaten

⅓ cup melted butter or vegetable oil

½ cup plus 1 tablespoon brown sugar

1½ cups all-purpose flour

1 teaspoon baking powder

½ teaspoon baking soda

½ teaspoon ground cinnamon

¼ teaspoon grated nutmeg

2 almost ripe peaches, pitted and flesh cut into large chunks

Greek yogurt, to serve (optional)

a deep 12-cup muffin pan, well greased

makes 12 muffins

Preheat the oven to 425°F.

Put the rolled oats and buttermilk in a large bowl and let soak for 10 minutes. Add the egg, melted butter, and sugar and mix well.

Sift the flour, baking powder, baking soda, and spices onto the soaked oat mixture and stir briefly. Quickly fold in the chopped peaches. The batter should look slightly streaky. Do not beat or overmix or the muffins will be tough and dry. Spoon the mixture into the prepared muffin pan, filling each cup about two-thirds full.

Bake in the preheated oven for 20–25 minutes, or until golden brown and firm to the touch. Let cool in the pan for 1 minute, then turn out onto a wire rack. Eat warm. The muffins should be eaten within 24 hours or left to cool, then frozen for up to 1 month.

Quick to make, these mouthwatering muffins can be baked several days in advance, then reheated in the oven briefly before serving. Use premium bittersweet chocolate, chopped up, rather than choc chips, as it has a much better flavor and texture.

pecan & chocolate muffins

1½ cups self-rising flour

1 teaspoon baking powder

2½ oz. pecans, finely ground

⅔ cup brown sugar

1 egg

¼ cup maple syrup

1 cup milk

4 tablespoons butter, melted

3½ oz. bittersweet chocolate, coarsely chopped into very small pieces

chopped pecans, to decorate

a 12-cup muffin pan, lined with paper cases

makes 12 muffins

Preheat the oven to 400°F.

Sift the flour and baking powder in a bowl, then stir in the ground pecans and sugar. Put the egg, maple syrup, milk, and melted butter into a second bowl and beat well. Beat the syrup mixture into the dry ingredients, then fold in the chocolate pieces.

Spoon the muffin mixture into the paper cases in the muffin pan, and sprinkle the surface of each muffin with extra chopped pecans.

Bake in the preheated oven for 18–20 minutes until risen and golden. Let cool in the pan for 1 minute, then turn out onto a wire rack. Eat warm. The muffins should be eaten within 24 hours or left to cool, then frozen for up to 1 month.

An all-time family favorite—who can resist these gooey, sticky caramel buns filled with cinnamon and nuts? They are so irresistible that you could eat them at any time of day, but midmorning with a fresh brew is the perfect occasion.

sticky buns

3½ cups white bread flour, sifted

1 teaspoon sea salt

2 tablespoons superfine sugar

1 cake compressed yeast (0.6 oz.)

7 fl oz. milk, lukewarm

6 tablespoons unsalted butter, melted

1 large egg, beaten

nut caramel filling

5 tablespoons soft unsalted butter

2 teaspoons ground cinnamon

⅓ cup light brown sugar

1 cup pecan or walnut pieces

sticky topping

½ cup plus 1 tablespoon light brown sugar

¼ cup heavy cream

a 9 x 11 x 2-inch baking or roasting pan, well greased

makes 12 buns

Mix the flour, salt, and sugar in a large bowl and make a well in the center. Crumble the yeast into another bowl, add the milk and stir until blended. Pour the yeast liquid into the well, then work in enough of the flour to make a thick batter. Cover the bowl with a kitchen towel and leave until foamy, thick and bubbly—about 15 minutes.

Add the butter and egg to the yeast mixture and work in the rest of the flour to make a soft but not sticky dough. If it is too dry or too sticky, add extra water or flour, 1 tablespoon at a time. Turn out onto a lightly floured surface and knead thoroughly for 10 minutes. Return the dough to the bowl and cover with a damp kitchen towel or put the bowl in an oiled plastic bag. Let rise at normal room temperature until doubled in size— about 1½ hours.

Knock down the risen dough with your knuckles, then turn out and roll into a rectangle, about 6 x 10 inches. To make the filling, beat the butter until creamy, then beat in the cinnamon and sugar. Spread the mixture over the dough leaving a ¼-inch border around the edges. Scatter the nuts over, then roll into a 16-inch-long roll. Cut into 12 equal pieces and space slightly apart in the pan, in 4 rows of 3. Cover and let rise as before until doubled in size—about 30 minutes (or chill overnight.)

Preheat the oven to 400°F. To make the topping, put all the ingredients in a small saucepan, bring to a boil, reduce the heat, and simmer for 1 minute. Pour the hot mixture over the buns. Bake for 25–30 minutes until golden and firm. Let cool in the pan for 10 minutes, then turn out carefully as the caramel will be hot. Let cool on a wire rack. Eat warm or at room temperature, within 24 hours.

Lazy weekend breakfasts are so good—it's that special feeling when time seems to stand still and the fast pace of weekday life slows right down. Why not start the day with a cup of tea or coffee in bed, then head to the kitchen to prepare one of these extra-special breakfast pastries?

plum pastries

1 can chilled ready-to-bake croissant dough, about 8 oz.

6 plums, halved and pitted

4 teaspoons honey

1 tablespoon slivered almonds

makes 6 pastries

Preheat the oven to 350°F.

Remove the dough from the pan, unravel it and flatten. Cut along the perforations to make 6 rectangles and lay well apart on a greased baking sheet.

Put 2 halves of fruit on each piece of pastry dough, then drizzle with honey and sprinkle with the almonds.

Bake in the preheated oven for 15–20 minutes until puffed and golden. Remove from the oven and serve hot or cold.

These rich, dark, chocolatey cakes studded with chocolate-covered coffee beans and topped with a creamy coffee butter frosting are simply divine. Dusted with grated chocolate, they look like a plateful of mini cappuccinos.

choca-mocha cupcakes

3½ oz. bittersweet chocolate

10 tablespoons butter, at room temperature

¾ cup granulated sugar

2 eggs

2 tablespoons cocoa powder

¾ cup self-rising flour

2 teaspoons instant coffee, dissolved in 1 tablespoon boiling water

¼ cup chocolate-covered coffee beans

grated bittersweet chocolate, to decorate

coffee butter frosting

7 tablespoons butter, at room temperature

1⅔ cups confectioners' sugar, sifted

2 teaspoons instant coffee, dissolved in 1 tablespoon boiling water

a 12-cup muffin pan, lined with paper cases

makes 12 cupcakes

Preheat the oven to 350°F.

Melt the chocolate in a heatproof bowl set over a saucepan of simmering water or in a microwave, then set aside to cool.

Beat the butter and sugar together in a bowl until pale and fluffy, then beat in the eggs, one at a time. Stir in the melted chocolate and cocoa powder. Sift the flour into the mixture and stir in, then stir in the dissolved coffee, followed by the coffee beans.

Spoon the mixture into the paper cases and bake for about 20 minutes until risen and a skewer inserted in the center comes out clean. Transfer to a wire rack to cool.

To decorate, beat the butter, confectioners' sugar, and dissolved coffee together in a bowl until pale and fluffy. Spread the mixture smoothly over the cakes and sprinkle with grated chocolate.

Here's a real treat for a special breakfast or one of those mornings when what you crave is a strong coffee, a slice of freshly baked cake, and a sit-down. They are so pretty that they are particularly good if you are expecting a couple of friends round for elevenses.

mini gingerbreads

1⅔ cups self-rising flour

1 teaspoon baking soda

1 tablespoon ground ginger

1 teaspoon apple pie spice

¼ teaspoon freshly grated nutmeg

¼ teaspoon ground cloves

1 stick unsalted butter, cubed

½ cup molasses

½ cup corn syrup

⅔ cup dark brown sugar

1¼ cups milk

1 extra-large egg, beaten

a 6-cup mini Bundt pan, greased
or a 8½ x 4½ x 2½-inch loaf pan,
greased and lined

makes 6 mini Bundt cakes or
1 loaf cake

Preheat the oven to 350°F.

Sift the flour, baking soda, ginger, apple pie spice, nutmeg, and cloves onto a sheet of wax paper, then tip into a food processor. Add the butter and process until the mixture looks like very fine crumbs.

Put the molasses, corn syrup, sugar, and milk in a pan and heat gently until the sugar dissolves. Cool until lukewarm, then, with the machine running, pour the mixture through the feed tube. Add the egg in the same way and process until just thoroughly mixed.

Spoon the mixture into the prepared Bundt pan until the cups are equally filled and bake for 20 minutes in the preheated oven, or until firm to the touch. Alternatively, if you are using a loaf pan, bake for 45–60 minutes, or until a skewer inserted into the center comes out clean.

Let cool for 15 minutes before unmolding onto a wire rack. Store in an airtight container and eat within 5 days.

An old-fashioned coffee cake, designed to serve with a cup of coffee (not made with it). When you cut a slice of this lovely cake, you reveal the layer of crunchy nut streusel hidden in the middle. A real treat.

traditional pecan
coffee cake

streusel

1 cup finely chopped pecans

¼ cup dark brown sugar

1½ teaspoons ground cinnamon

batter

2 sticks plus 1 tablespoon unsalted butter, softened

2 extra-large eggs, at room temperature, beaten

¾ cup superfine sugar

1 cup sour cream

2 cups all-purpose flour

½ teaspoon baking soda

2 teaspoons baking powder

a good pinch of salt

confectioners' sugar, to dust

a 7½-inch diameter Bundt pan, well greased,or a 8½ x 4½ x 2½-inch loaf pan, greased and lined

makes 1 Bundt or loaf cake

Preheat the oven to 350°F.

To make the streusel mixture, mix the pecans, sugar, and cinnamon in a small bowl and set aside.

To make the batter, put the butter, eggs, sugar, and sour cream in a large bowl and beat with an electric mixer on medium speed until smooth and well blended.

Sift the flour, baking soda, baking powder, and salt onto the mixture and mix in gently.

Spoon half the batter into the prepared Bundt or loaf pan and spread it evenly with a rubber spatula. Sprinkle with half of the streusel mixture. Spoon the rest of the batter into the pan and spread evenly. Sprinkle with the remaining streusel, then gently press the mixture onto the surface of the batter with the back of a spoon.

Bake in the preheated oven for 45–55 minutes or until a skewer inserted in the thickest part of the cake comes out clean. Remove the cake from the oven and let cool in the pan, on a wire cooling rack. Let cool completely, then invert onto a serving platter. Dust with confectioners' sugar before serving. Store in an airtight container and eat within 4 days.

Coffee and walnuts are wonderful together. Drizzling the nutty cake with a spiced coffee syrup leaves it deliciously moist and gooey. This cake is equally at home as a dessert for a dinner party as it is midmorning for a quick treat.

walnut cake
with coffee syrup

6 eggs, separated

¾ cup superfine sugar

2½ cups walnut halves, finely ground

¾ cup day-old bread crumbs

whipped cream, to serve

coffee syrup

1¼ cups strong black coffee

½ cup superfine sugar

3 star anise

a 9-inch spring form cake pan, greased and lined with parchment paper

serves 8

Preheat the oven to 350°F.

Put the egg yolks in a large bowl, add ⅔ cup of the sugar, and beat until pale. Stir in the ground walnuts and bread crumbs. (The mixture will be very stiff at this stage.)

Beat the egg whites in a separate bowl until soft peaks form, then gradually beat in the remaining sugar. Stir a large spoonful of the beaten egg whites into the cake mixture, then fold in the rest until evenly mixed. Spoon into the prepared cake pan and bake in the preheated oven for 35–40 minutes, or until risen and springy to the touch. Remove from the oven and leave the cake in the pan.

Meanwhile, to make the coffee syrup, put the coffee, sugar, and star anise in a saucepan. Heat until the sugar dissolves, then boil for 5–6 minutes, or until syrupy. Let cool slightly.

Using a wooden toothpick, spike the cake all over the surface, then drizzle with half the syrup. Set aside to cool slightly. Serve the cake still warm with lightly whipped cream and the remaining coffee syrup spooned around it in a pool.

Light and crumbly in texture and crammed with delicious fruit and nuts—irresistible. Use very ripe bananas for maximum flavor. This loaf also works well as a sweet treat for the children when they come home from school.

banana pecan loaf

1 stick unsalted butter,
at room temperature

¾ cup sugar

2 large eggs, beaten

½ teaspoon vanilla extract

3 small very ripe bananas

1 cup pecans, coarsely sliced

2 cups less 1 tablespoon self-rising

flour, sifted

a 9½ x 5½ x 3½-inch loaf pan, greased and lined with baking parchment

makes 1 large loaf cake

Preheat the oven to 350°F.

Using an electric mixer or wooden spoon, beat the butter with the sugar until light and creamy. Gradually beat in the eggs and vanilla extract to make a fluffy mixture. Mash the bananas with a fork—they should be fairly coarse rather than a purée. Carefully fold in the mashed bananas, pecans, and flour. Transfer the mixture to the prepared loaf pan and smooth the surface with a spatula. Bake in the preheated oven for about 1 hour, or until golden and firm to the touch and a skewer inserted into the center comes out clean.

Let cool in the pan for 5 minutes, then turn out onto a wire rack to cool completely. Serve warm or at room temperature, thickly sliced and spread with butter. The cake is best eaten within 3 days. It can be frozen for up to 1 month.

For a full tea flavor, use a strong variety such as an English breakfast or Irish blend, or a rich malty Assam. Eat the loaf cake thickly sliced, warm or even toasted, with or without butter and jam. It really is good enough to eat on its own.

breakfast tea loaf

2 cups all-bran cereal

⅔ cup dark brown sugar

1 cup mix of raisins, golden raisins, and currants

¾ cup freshly-brewed tea, warm

⅓ cup walnut pieces

¾ cup all-purpose flour, sifted

1½ teaspoons baking powder

1½ teaspoons apple pie spice

an 8½ x 4½ x 2½-inch loaf pan, greased and lined with baking parchment

makes 1 medium tea loaf

Put the cereal, sugar, and dried fruit into a large bowl, add the warm tea, stir well, then cover and let soak for 30 minutes.

Preheat the oven to 350°F.

Add the remaining ingredients and stir with a wooden spoon until thoroughly mixed. (The cereal will disappear into the mixture.)

Spoon the mixture into the prepared loaf pan and smooth the surface with a spatula. Bake in the preheated oven for about 45 minutes, or until firm and well risen and a skewer inserted into the center comes out clean.

Let cool in the pan until lukewarm, then turn out and eat while still warm. Alternatively, turn out onto a wire rack to cool completely.

Eat within 4 days, or freeze for up to 1 month.

Great for a fast, simple breakfast—on its own or toasted and buttered. Cinnamon, raisins, and nuts are a classic combination. Make this on the weekend and enjoy your homemade breakfast bread every morning for the next few days.

cinnamon raisin nut bread

4 cups unbleached white bread flour

1½ tablespoons ground cinnamon

1 teaspoon sea salt

1 teaspoon light brown sugar

7 tablespoons unsalted butter, chilled and cubed

1 cake compressed yeast (0.6 oz.)

1¾ cups milk, at room temperature

⅔ cup raisins

¾ cup walnut pieces, lightly toasted

makes 1 large round loaf

Sift the flour, cinnamon, salt, and sugar into a large bowl. Rub in the butter with your fingertips until the mixture looks like fine crumbs, then make a well in the center. Crumble the yeast into a pitcher and beat in the milk. Pour into the well and mix in enough flour to make a thick batter. Cover the bowl and leave until thick and foamy—about 20 minutes.

Work in the rest of the flour to make a soft but not sticky dough. If it is too dry or too sticky, add extra water or flour, 1 tablespoon at a time. Turn out onto a floured surface and knead thoroughly for 10 minutes, or until smooth and elastic. Return to the bowl, cover with a damp kitchen towel and let rise at normal room temperature until doubled in size—about 1½ hours.

Punch down the risen dough with your knuckles, then work in the raisins and nuts, kneading until thoroughly mixed. Shape the dough into an oval loaf about 10 x 6 inches. Put on a greased baking sheet, cover and let rise as before until doubled in size—about 45 minutes.

Preheat the oven to 425°F.

Bake in the preheated oven for about 35 minutes, or until the bread is nicely browned and sounds hollow when tapped underneath. Let cool on a wire rack. Eat within 4 days, or slice and toast. The cooled loaf can be frozen for up to 1 month.

To get the best results for this recipe (and to feel virtuous), use a good sugarless granola with ingredients such as raisins, dates, wheat flakes, oat flakes, apples, apricots, hazelnuts, almonds, and raisins.

granola round

3½ cups white bread flour, plus extra for dusting

⅔ cup stone-ground whole-wheat flour

1⅔ cups unsweetened granola

2 teaspoons salt

1 cake compressed yeast (0.6 oz.), crumbled

about 1¾ cups milk and water equal mixture, at room temperature

1 tablespoon honey

2 tablespoons vegetable oil

makes 1 large round loaf

Put the flours, granola, and salt in a large bowl and mix well. Make a well in the center.

Put the yeast and 3 tablespoons of the milk mixture in a small bowl and cream to a smooth liquid. Stir in the rest of the liquid, the honey, and oil, then pour into the well in the flour.

Gradually mix the dry ingredients into the liquid to make a fairly firm dough. If it seems dry or stiff, or there are dry crumbs in the bottom of the bowl, work in extra milk or water, 1 tablespoon at a time. If the dough sticks to your fingers, knead in extra white flour, 1 tablespoon at a time. The amount of liquid needed will depend on the granola mix.

Transfer the dough to a lightly floured work surface and knead for about 5 minutes. Return the dough to the bowl, cover with a damp kitchen towel and leave at room temperature until doubled in size—1–1½ hours. Turn out the dough onto a lightly floured work surface and knead for 1 minute. Shape into a round loaf 8 inches across. Put on a greased baking sheet and score into 8 segments with a very sharp knife. Cover and let rise as before—about 1 hour.

Preheat the oven to 425°F.

Uncover the loaf and sprinkle with bread flour. Bake in the preheated oven for 30 minutes, or until it sounds hollow when tapped underneath. Remove from the oven and transfer to a wire rack to cool.

Eat warm, spread with butter and lots of apricot preserve, pear and ginger jam, or apple marmalade—a good start to the day. These are so good you'll wonder why you only ever ate scones at teatime!

apple buttermilk scone round

1 large baking apple or 1–2 crisp tart eating apples (about ½ lb.)

1¾ cups all-purpose flour, plus extra for dusting

¾ cup whole-wheat flour

1 teaspoon baking soda

½ cup raw sugar, plus extra for sprinkling

6½ tablespoons unsalted butter, chilled and cubed

about ⅔ cup buttermilk, plus extra for brushing

makes 8 scones

Preheat the oven to 425°F.

Peel, core, and coarsely chop the apple into ½-inch chunks. Mix the flours, baking soda, and sugar in a food processor. Add the butter and process until the mixture looks like fine crumbs. With the machine running, add the buttermilk through the feed tube to make a soft but not sticky dough.

Turn out onto a floured surface and knead in the apple chunks to form a coarse and bumpy dough. Shape into a ball and put in the middle of a greased baking sheet. With floured fingers, pat into a 9-inch round. Brush lightly with buttermilk to glaze, then sprinkle with a little raw sugar to give a crunchy surface. Using a sharp knife, score the round into 8 wedges. Bake in the preheated oven for 20–25 minutes, or until lightly golden and firm to the touch.

Remove from the oven and let cool on a wire rack. Eat warm, immediately or within 24 hours. The scones are also good split and toasted. They can be frozen for up to 1 month.

Scottish cooks are famous throughout Britain for their baking skills, and scones (biscuits) are perhaps their finest achievement. Mashed potato is used to replace some of the flour here, giving a light, moist texture, and the Parmesan and pancetta give an Italian twist.

golden potato biscuits
with parmesan & pancetta

4 slices of pancetta or smoked bacon, about 2 oz., cut into small pieces

1⅛ cups all-purpose flour

2 teaspoons baking powder

½ teaspoon salt

4 tablespoons unsalted butter, cubed

½ cup cooked mashed potato

2 oz. Parmesan cheese, cut into tiny cubes

1 teaspoon dried oregano

about 2 tablespoons milk

1 egg yolk, beaten, to glaze

a fluted 2½-inch cookie cutter

makes 10 scones

Preheat the oven to 425°F.

Heat a skillet and dry-fry the pancetta for 5–6 minutes, or until crispy. Remove with a slotted spoon and let cool on paper towels.

Sift the flour, baking powder, and salt together in a large bowl. Add the butter and rub in until the mixture resembles bread crumbs.

Add the potato, Parmesan, oregano, and cooked pancetta and mix well. Add enough milk to form a soft but firm dough, tip out onto a lightly floured work surface and knead briefly. Roll out the dough to ½ inch thick and, using the cookie cutter, stamp out 2½-inch rounds. Re-roll any trimmings and cut more rounds, to make about 10 in total.

Place the biscuits on a well-greased baking sheet, brush the tops with the beaten egg and bake for 10–15 minutes, or until golden brown and well risen. Let cool a little on a wire rack, then serve while still warm, spread with unsalted butter.

Hot or cold, these make a great snack either midmorning or midafternoon. Top with cottage cheese, cream cheese, hummus, or sliced tomatoes and basil.

herby cheese swirls

1 cup whole-wheat flour

2 teaspoons baking powder

¼ cup unprocessed oat bran

2 tablespoons polyunsaturated margarine, cubed

½ cup milk

2 oz. fat-reduced cheddar cheese, grated

1 tablespoon chopped fresh flat leaf parsley

2 tablespoons chopped fresh basil

2 teaspoons chopped fresh rosemary

to serve (optional)

cottage cheese

cream cheese

hummus

tomato slices and fresh basil leaves

makes 10 swirls

Preheat the oven to 400°F.

Sift the flour and the baking powder in a large bowl, then stir in the oat bran. Rub in the margarine using your fingertips. The mixture should resemble bread crumbs. Make a well in the center and add the milk and 2 tablespoons water. Mix lightly with a round-bladed knife, adding extra water if necessary, to make a soft, pliable dough. Do not overmix.

Turn the dough out onto a lightly floured surface and knead gently. Roll out to a rectangle about ⅛ inch thick. Scatter half the cheese and all the herbs evenly over the surface, then dampen the edges of the dough with water. Beginning from one long side, roll up the dough like a jelly roll, to make a thick sausage shape. Carefully cut into 1¼-inch slices using a sharp knife, to make about 10 rounds.

Transfer the rounds to a baking sheet, spacing them well apart. Sprinkle with the remaining cheese and bake for 15–20 minutes, until golden. Serve hot or cold, either plain or with your choice of topping.

perfect preserves

This is a quintessentially British preserve, tart with lemon yet sweet and buttery. It is delicious on toast or freshly made tea loaf or scones. It is easy to make so long as you stir it very frequently and keep the heat low so that the water in the pan barely bubbles.

lemon curd

2 large lemons

1 stick unsalted butter, cubed

1 cup superfine sugar

3 eggs, beaten

2 x 8-oz. glass jars

makes 2 small jars

Finely grate the zest from the lemons into a heatproof bowl. Squeeze the juice and add that to the bowl with the butter and sugar.

Place the bowl over a pan of just-simmering water, making sure the water doesn't touch the base of the bowl. Stir until the butter melts, add the egg and, using a wooden spoon, stir for 10–15 minutes until the mixture thickens noticeably and takes on a translucent look.

For a very smooth preserve, strain the curd through a fine sieve into a measuring pitcher, then pot it into small, sterilized jars (see page 4.) Cover with plastic wrap or waxed paper when cold. It will keep for 15 days in the refrigerator.

variations:

lime & cardamom curd

Substitute the zest of 3 large limes and the freshly squeezed juice of 5 limes for the lemons above. Add ¼ teaspoon finely ground cardamom pods to the butter and sugar as it melts.

passion fruit & lime curd

Use the zest of 1 large lime, the freshly squeezed juice of 2 limes and the sieved pulp of 8 ripe passion fruit (heating the pulp gently in the microwave for a few seconds makes it easier to sieve.) Add 1–2 teaspoons of the passion fruit seeds at the end for crunch.

Apricots make one of the most luxurious preserves of all. The apricot season is fairly short so this recipe using dried apricots is very useful. Dried apricots need soaking well, then long, slow cooking to soften them.

dried apricot conserve

2½ cups dried apricots
(soaked weight 2 lb.)

freshly squeezed juice of 1 lemon

5 cups sugar

⅓ cup walnut halves, broken into
4 pieces

2 tablespoons Amaretto liqueur
(optional)

4 x ½-pint glass jars

waxed paper disks

makes about 1 quart conserve

Cut the apricots in half, put in a large bowl, cover with cold water, add the lemon juice and set aside for 24 hours.

Strain off the juice into a measuring cup and make up to 1 quart with cold water. Put the fruit in a heavy-bottomed pan, add the juice and water and simmer over low heat for 30 minutes or until quite soft. The fruit can be mashed at this stage or left in pieces.

Add the sugar and bring slowly to simmering point. Cook gently, stirring until dissolved. Increase the heat and boil hard for 10 minutes, add the walnut pieces and return to a fast boil.

Remove the pan from the heat and let stand while you test for set (see below.) If the jam is not ready, put the pan back on the heat to boil for a few minutes longer and test again. Repeat this process if necessary and remember to take the jam off the heat while testing, because over-boiling will ruin it.

When setting point has been reached, add the Amaretto to the pan, if using. Return to a boil, stir, and skim if necessary. Let the jam rest for 20 minutes, then stir well and ladle into sterilized jars (see page 4.) Seal at once with waxed paper disks and lids or covers. Let cool, label, and store in a cool, dark pantry.

testing for set:

Before you start making jam, always put a saucer and 2–3 teaspoons in the refrigerator to cool. Boil the reduced preserve hard for 5 minutes, then take the pan off the heat and test for set. Take a teaspoon of the preserve, put it on the cold saucer in the refrigerator or freezer and leave for 5 minutes. Push it with a finger—if it offers resistance or crinkles, it is ready.

There is no boiling needed for this recipe, so you keep the taste of fresh raspberries. Commercially produced "jam sugar" is perfect for this—it has added pectin that helps the jam thicken to a soft set. Use ½ cup liquid pectin if you can't find this special jam sugar.

uncooked freezer
raspberry jam

1½ lb. fresh raspberries

5 cups sugar with added pectin (sometimes known as "jam sugar")

2 tablespoons freshly squeezed lemon juice

2 x 16-oz glass jars

makes 2 large jars

Tip the raspberries into a bowl and mash a bit with a potato masher. Stir in the jam sugar and lemon juice. Cover with plastic wrap and heat on medium in the microwave for about 5 minutes, or until warmed through thoroughly.

Uncover and stir gently to dissolve the sugar, then let stand overnight. Alternatively, heat in a saucepan until the sugar has dissolved.

The next day, pot up into freezer containers and freeze—keep one pot in the refrigerator for breakfast tomorrow. After removing from the freezer, store the jam in the refrigerator. Thaw before using.

The beauty of this marmalade is that it can be made in small quantities at any time of the year, not just when Seville oranges are in season. Cut the peel to suit your taste—thick or thin by hand, chunky, or fine using a blender.

chunky lemon, lime, & grapefruit
marmalade

1 lemon

1 small pink grapefruit

1 lime

5 cups sugar

freshly squeezed juice of ½ lemon

3 x ½-pint jars

waxed paper disks

makes 1½ pints marmalade

Scrub the fruit and prise out any stalk ends. Put in a pan and cover with 2 cups cold water. Set over low heat and cook until tender—1½–2 hours. The fruit is ready when it "collapses." Lime zest is much tougher than other citrus peel, so you must make sure it is tender at this stage.

Transfer the fruit to a cutting board and leave until cool enough to handle. Cut in half, scrape out all the flesh and pips, and add to the pan of water. Bring to a boil and simmer for 5 minutes. Cut the zest into strips, or put it in a blender and blend until chunky. Strain the water from the pips and flesh and return it to the pan, adding the chopped zest and the lemon juice. Discard the pips and debris.

Add the sugar to the pan and bring slowly to simmering point, stirring until the sugar has dissolved. Because the sugar content is high, this will take quite a long time. When the marmalade has become translucent, you will know the sugar has dissolved and you can increase the heat. Bring to a boil and boil rapidly until setting point is reached—5–10 minutes.

Take the pan off the heat and test for set (see page 193.) If the marmalade is not ready, put the pan back on the heat to boil for a few minutes longer and test again. Repeat this process if necessary and remember to take the pan off the heat during testing because over-boiling will ruin it.

When setting point has been reached, return to simmering point, then turn off of the heat. Skim with a perforated skimmer, stir well, and leave to stand for 30 minutes. Stir and ladle into sterilized jars (see page 4). Seal with waxed paper disks and cover with a lid.

Let cool, label, and store in a cool, dark pantry.

This is a robust jam that deserves a place alongside the zingiest of marmalades. Choose young pink rhubarb if possible, because it will give a lovely pink color to the jam—green rhubarb tends to turn brown when cooked.

rhubarb & ginger jam

3 lb. young rhubarb, pink if possible

7½ cups sugar

grated zest and freshly squeezed juice of 1½ lemons

1–1½ oz. fresh ginger, peeled, to taste

3–4 x ½-pint glass jars

waxed paper disks

makes about 1 quart jam

Wipe the rhubarb, trim it, cut into chunks, and put in a bowl with the sugar, lemon zest, and juice. Cover and let stand overnight.

Crush the ginger with a mortar and pestle or blender and add to the fruit and sugar. Transfer to a large pan and bring slowly to simmering point, stirring all the time to dissolve the sugar. Simmer gently until the fruit has softened, then increase the heat and boil rapidly for 5–10 minutes until setting point is reached (see page 193.)

If the jam is not ready, put the pan back on the heat to a boil for a few minutes longer and test again. Repeat this process if necessary and remember to take the jam off the heat while testing, because over-boiling will ruin it.

Skim with a perforated skimmer, stir well and let stand for 20 minutes. Stir and ladle into sterilized jars (see page 4), seal with waxed paper disks, and cover with a lid. Let cool, label, and store in a cool, dark pantry.

variation: Rhubarb combines well with soft fruit such as blackcurrants, raspberries, and strawberries, giving them more body and reducing the seediness of the fruit. Use half soft fruit and half rhubarb, and leave out the ginger.

Make sure you use only plump, firm fruit here. You can use green figs, but they should be peeled first. It is perfect with crusty bread and butter, brioche, or toast for breakfast, but would also make excellent jam tartlets or Italian *crostata*.

italian fig conserve

3 lb. firm black Mission figs

freshly squeezed juice of 2 lemons

6 cups sugar

½ tablespoon vanilla extract (optional)

3–4 x ½-pint glass jars

waxed paper disks

makes about 1 quart conserve

Wipe the figs and chop into tiny pieces. Put in a saucepan with the lemon juice and 1 cup water. Cook over low heat until soft—this may take about 20–30 minutes, but if the skins are not cooked until tender at this stage, they will be tough when boiled with the sugar. Add the sugar and cook over low heat until dissolved. Stir in the vanilla, increase the heat, and boil until setting point is reached (see page 193)—5–10 minutes.

If the jam is not ready, put the pan back on the heat to boil for a few minutes longer and test again. Repeat this process if necessary and remember to take the jam off the heat while testing, because over-boiling will ruin it.

When setting point has been reached, skim with a perforated skimmer, stir well and let stand for 20 minutes. Stir and ladle into sterilized jars (see page 4), seal with waxed paper disks and cover with a lid. Let cool, label, and store in a cool, dark pantry.

variation: Try experimenting with peaches, nectarines, and kiwi fruit, although it may not be necessary to cook the fruit for so long.

Berries make a marvellous seedless jam—use sweet ones like strawberries and raspberries, blackberry-raspberry crosses like the Scottish tayberry or the Californian loganberry, then something sharp such as cranberries, red currants, or black currants.

red berry jelly

1 lb. strawberries

1 lb. raspberries or red currants

1 lb. loganberries or tayberries

1 lb. black currants

freshly squeezed juice of 1 lemon

sugar or preserving sugar (see method)

a jelly bag or cheesecloth

2–3 x ½-pint glass jars

waxed paper disks

makes 1–1½ pints jelly

Put all the fruit in a large preserving pan with the lemon juice and 2 cups water and bring slowly to a boil. Partially cover with a lid and simmer until the fruit has softened—10–15 minutes. Transfer to a jelly bag or cheesecloth suspended over a large bowl and let drip overnight.

Measure the juice into a clean preserving pan and, for every 1 cup of juice, add 1 scant cup of sugar. Set over low heat and bring to simmering point, dissolving the sugar, stirring all the time. When it has dissolved, increase the heat and boil hard for 5–10 minutes until setting point is reached (see page 193.)

When setting point has been reached, skim with a perforated skimmer and stir well. Stir and ladle into sterilized jars (see page 4), seal with waxed paper disks, and cover with a lid. Let cool, label, and store in a cool, dark pantry.

delicious drinks

On many mornings for a lot of people, a cup of coffee simply IS breakfast. Whether you belong to this minimalist school, or coffee is just one essential ingredient of a larger meal, do forgo a convenient but watery cup of instant and take the time to prepare it properly.

coffee

To really taste the full, fresh, and interesting flavors coffee can offer, you must make it correctly. Whether you are making espresso (when hot water is forced under pressure through dark-roasted coffee to extract maximum flavor), or using some sort of filter, follow these four principles and you won't go far wrong:

1 Buy good-quality, freshly roasted whole beans and grind them only just before using. Store whole beans in a dark airtight container, in a cool pantry rather than in the refrigerator.

2 How finely you grind them depends on what method you are using to make the coffee:

espresso (including in stove-top pots): finely ground

cafetière: coarsely ground

filter: (by hand, machine, drip pots, or vacuum pots): medium-finely ground

jug: coarsely ground

3 Be precise in your measurements. Getting the proper proportion of coffee to water and allowing them to brew together for the right length of time ensures you extract the most character and aromatic oils from the beans without the brew becoming bitter. To make weaker coffee, add hot water when it has brewed correctly, rather than using too few beans in the first place.

When making espresso, fill the coffee container to the brim and do not compress the grounds, but level them off gently, otherwise the water will not be able to get through it evenly. Fill with water to the mark or rivet (depending on the design of your espresso maker).

For filter coffee, use 2 tablespoons coffee per ⅔ cup water, and brew it for 6–8 minutes to extract the full flavor from the beans.

4 Pour the water onto the grounds when it is just off the boil. This is to coax the soluble flavors from the coffee rather than scalding it and turning it bitter. Middle Eastern coffee is the exception, since this is boiled. As a general rule, do not keep coffee warm on the heat or it will become bitter and stewed. Instead, wrap the pot in a kitchen towel while it infuses to keep it warm. Do not reheat previously brewed coffee, for the same reason.

Tea is a real chameleon of a drink. From a fortifying cup of regular tea to a cleansing and almost spiritual cup of green tea, there are forms and flavors to suit everyone and all occasions. Many, justifiably, consider their morning incomplete without it.

tea

Whether you drink it with or without milk or lemon and sugar is a matter of choice and tea variety, but as with coffee, there are certain principles to follow to ensure you get the best flavor from your tea. Many tea varieties are now available in tea bag form. While some are of reasonable quality, proper leaf tea is in a different league. To guarantee the best cup, follow these guidelines:

1 Buy top-quality tea leaves and store them in an airtight container to maintain freshness.

2 Use a tea pot. Keep the pot clean by rinsing it in detergent-free hot water after use to prevent a build-up of tannin, which will spoil future brews. Do not wash it in the dishwasher.

3 Fill the kettle with freshly drawn cold water and boil it. Do not use reheated water as it contains less oxygen and will give the tea a stale taste.

4 Warm the tea pot with hot water, then empty it. This ensures the boiling water is not cooled when it hits the leaves, and encourages the leaves to open properly.

5 Allow 1 heaped teaspoon tea leaves per person and 1 for the pot. Let the tea brew, and stir before pouring. Steep green teas for 3 minutes, and black and oolong teas for up to 5 minutes. Longer than this and your tea will taste stewed. If you like it weaker, taste after 2 minutes, and then at 2-minute intervals until it suits. Pour into the cup through a strainer.

herbal & fruit teas

For those concerned about stimulants, but in need of a low-cal hot drink, caffeine-free alternatives in the form of herbal and fruit teas are also popular. Many of these have specific additional benefits for health and well-being, such as digestive mint, memory-sharpening rosemary, and soothing chamomile.

Many of us know the benefits of a citrus kick to get us going in the morning. When the sun is shining on a gorgeous summer day, make this refreshing Iced Lime Tea to accompany your al-fresco breakfast. When it is wet, windy, and cold, swap it for a cup of Hot Lemon Tea instead.

iced lime tea

1 quart freshly made tea, lightly brewed

sugar, to taste

1–2 unwaxed limes, finely sliced

ice cubes

sparkling mineral water, lemonade, or ginger ale

serves 4

Strain the tea into a pitcher, stir in enough sugar to taste, let cool, then chill. Put sliced limes into a serving pitcher, then half-fill it with ice cubes. Half-fill the pitcher with the cold tea, then top up with sparkling mineral water, lemonade, or ginger ale, stir, and serve.

hot lemon tea

1 unwaxed lemon

1 tablespoon honey

1 pot of tea

serves 1

Cut 2 slices off the lemon and squeeze the juice from the rest. Put the honey and sliced lemon into a large cup, add the lemon juice, then top with tea. Stir and drink.

When you have indulged in an especially hearty breakfast or brunch, finish it off with a cup of this supremely soothing Mint Tea. Mint aids the digestion, so will guarantee satisfaction with your meal.

mint tea

a large bunch of fresh mint

sugar or honey, to taste (optional)

1 tablespoon green tea (optional)

serves 1–4

Break the mint into large handfuls and put into a cafetière.

Pour over boiling water, leave to steep for 3–5 minutes, then press the plunger. Pour into tea glasses, add honey, if using, and a few fresh mint leaves, then serve. If using green tea, add it at the same time as the mint.

Any apples will do for this juice, but Granny Smiths produce the most beautiful green. The ginger is optional but utterly delicious. The apple is a good source of Vitamin C while the mint helps digestion and the ginger will calm an upset stomach.

minty ginger granny smith

4 Granny Smiths, cored but not peeled, then cut into chunks

a chunk of fresh ginger, peeled and sliced (optional)

4–8 sprigs of fresh mint

1 tablespoon freshly squeezed lime juice

serves 1

Blend half the apples in a juicer or blender (adding a little water if necessary to make the blades turn), then add the ginger, mint, and lime juice. Finally, add the remaining apples.

Tisane is a French word which means an infusion of herbs, flowers, or leaves, usually dried—a kind of tea, in other words. In early times, they were seen as cures for many ailments. A tisanière is a tall, lidded cup, with a strainer inside to hold the herb. If you don't have one, you can use a cafetière instead.

rosemary tisane

4–6 sprigs of fresh rosemary

1–2 teaspoons honey

serves 1–2

Put the rosemary and honey into a tisanière or cafetière and cover with boiling water. Let infuse for 5 minutes, then plunge or strain.

variations: Tisanes can also be made with chamomile flowers, lemon balm, marjoram, sage, thyme, and orange blossoms.

Fresh pineapple contains the enzyme bromelian, which helps with digestion so it's a good fruit to have as a juice at the start of the day. It makes short work of fats and proteins, so is very good for dieters. It is also soothing for sore throats, coughs, and upset stomachs.

pineapple crush

1 large pineapple

freshly squeezed juice of 1 lemon

ice cubes

4 passion fruit (optional)

sugar or honey, to taste

serves 4

Put the pineapple and lemon juice in a blender or juicer and blitz. Pour into a pitcher of ice. Stir in the flesh and seeds of 3 passion fruit and top with the remainder. Depending on the sweetness and ripeness of the pineapple, you may like to add a little sugar or honey.

Orange juice used in juices and smoothies will help to extend more expensive fruits and their gentle acidity also develops the flavor. Use juice you have squeezed fresh from the oranges rather than commercial juice which is often pasteurized, destroying all the Vitamin C and replacing it with ascorbic acid.

blueberry & orange smoothie

freshly squeezed juice of 4 oranges

2½ cups blueberries

sugar (optional)

serves 1–2

Put the orange juice into a blender, add the blueberries, and blend until smooth. Add sugar to taste, if using.

berry, apricot, & orange slush

8 ripe apricots, halved and pitted, then coarsely chopped

8 strawberries, hulled and halved

freshly squeezed juice of 2 oranges

serves 1

Put the apricots, strawberries, and orange juice into a blender and purée until smooth, adding water if needed. (If the mixture is too thick, add a little water and blend again.)

note: If you prefer, you can remove the apricot skins before blending. To do so, bring a saucepan of water to a boil, then blanch the apricots for about 1 minute. Remove the skin with the back of a knife.

Fruit and yogurt drinks are packed full of goodness and vitality and could almost be served as a meal in themselves. When really ripe mangoes are unavailable, canned mango purée, available from Asian stores, makes an easy alternative. But ripe fresh mangoes are best—they are good for the skin and for people with high blood pressure.

raspberry & rosewater lassi

2 cups raspberries

4 tablespoons rosewater

1¼ cups plain yogurt

2–3 tablespoons honey

12 ice cubes

serves 4

Put all the ingredients in a blender. Blend to a purée. If your blender doesn't crush ice, add it at the end.

mango, coconut, & passion fruit shake

1 large mango, peeled, or 1¼ cups mango purée

6 large passion fruit, or scant ⅔ cup passion fruit juice

¾ cup coconut milk

12 ice cubes

serves 4

Cut the mango flesh away from the pit. Coarsely chop the flesh and put into a blender. Cut the passion fruit in half and scoop the seeds into a strainer placed over a bowl. Use a spoon to press down the seeds and extract all the juice. Add the juice, coconut milk, and ice cubes to the blender and purée until smooth and creamy. If your blender doesn't crush ice, add it at the end.

Even people with a dairy intolerance are often able to eat yogurt, since it changes its structure during fermentation—it's marvellous for upset stomachs too—so this is a lovely, satisfying drink to fill you up for the morning.

red berry smoothie

about 8 oz berries, such as strawberries, cranberries, red currants, or raspberries (for a pink smoothie), or blackberries and blueberries (for a blue smoothie)

1 cup plain yogurt

½ cup crushed ice

sugar or honey, to taste

serves 2–3

Put all the ingredients into a blender and work to a thin, frothy cream. If your blender doesn't crush ice, add it at the end. If the smoothie is too thick, add a little water and blend again.

Taste, then add sugar or honey if you prefer.

Either of these will make a refreshing breakfast alternative. The Banana and Honey Breakfast Smoothie is packed with calcium and fiber and very good for you. The Watermelon and Lime Slush is a real taste of summer sunshine.

watermelon & lime slush

red flesh from 1 round watermelon

a chunk of fresh ginger, grated

to serve

2 limes, cut into wedges

crushed ice

serves 4

Press the melon flesh and ginger through a juicer, then pour into a pitcher half full of crushed ice. Serve immediately in glasses with lime wedges.

banana & honey breakfast smoothie

1 cup milk

1 cup yogurt

2 tablespoons crushed ice

1 tablespoon honey

1 banana

1 tablespoon wheatgerm

serves 2–4

Put all the ingredients into a blender and blend until smooth. If your blender doesn't crush ice, add it at the end. Add extra fruit if you wish.

These smoothies are fantastic because they will pep you up and their vibrant colors alone will put a smile on your face. Packed with fresh fruit, their lovely fresh, clean flavors will gently awaken your taste buds so they're a great way of making sure you and your family get the benefit of all the healthy nutrients that fruit contains.

carrot, apple, & ginger smoothie

5 large carrots, peeled

5 apples, cored

1 inch fresh ginger, peeled

serves 2

Press all the ingredients through a juicer or blitz in a blender (with a little water if necessary to make the blades turn). Serve immediately.

raspberry, kiwi, & blueberry smoothie

2 cups raspberries, fresh or frozen (no need to thaw)

2 kiwi fruit, peeled

2 cups blueberries, fresh or frozen

¾ cup milk

serves 2

Put everything in a blender and blitz until smooth. Adjust the consistency with more milk if you wish, and serve immediately.

Bananas and papayas won't juice effectively—their pulp is too dense—but they are definitely candidates for the blender treatment. Bananas are high in complex carbohydrates, very nourishing, and good for your cholesterol levels.

banana & papaya smoothie

1 small papaya, peeled, seeded, and cut into chunks

1 banana, peeled and cut into chunks

1 cup ice

1 tablespoon wheatgerm (optional)

½ cup yogurt or water (optional)

serves 2–4

Put the papaya and banana into a blender with the ice and the yogurt or water, if using. If your blender doesn't crush ice, add it at the end. Blend until smooth, then add the wheatgerm, if using, and extra water or yogurt to form a pourable consistency, then serve.

variation: Blueberries and banana make a famously good combination. Blend them with ice, yogurt, and a dash of honey.

There is something decidedly decadent about a glass of fizz in the morning. It's an absolute must if you're going to treat yourself to brunch, particularly if it's a special occasion, such as a birthday or an anniversary. Even if it's not, why not totally spoil yourself with one of these cocktails based on sparkling wine?

campari fizz

6 oz. Campari

3 teaspoons sugar

1 bottle chilled sparkling wine, 750 ml

serves 6

Pour the Campari into champagne flutes and stir ½ teaspoon sugar into each glass. Top up with sparkling wine and serve.

peach bellini

3 ripe peaches

1 bottle chilled Prosecco or sparkling wine, 750 ml

serves 6

Peel the peaches by plunging them into boiling water for 30 seconds. Refresh them under cold water and peel off the skin. Cut in half, remove the pit, and chop the flesh.

Put the peaches into a blender, add a small amount of Prosecco, and process to a purée. Pour into glasses, top up with the remaining Prosecco, and serve.

mimosa

6 blood or ordinary oranges

1 bottle chilled sparkling wine, 750 ml

serves 6

Squeeze the oranges and divide the juice between 6 glasses. Top up with wine and serve.

When tomato juice is on the menu for breakfast, you clearly mean business. If you can't face alcohol this early in the day, make the Virgin Mary which is a safer breakfast option. Sometimes, however, you need a real kickstart—which is when you should mix the more potent, alcoholic recipe and get on with the rest of the day.

kickstarter bloody mary

5 lemons

1 cup vodka

3 inches white horseradish, freshly grated, or 1 tablespoon horseradish sauce

1 tablespoon Worcestershire sauce

1 teaspoon Tabasco sauce

lots of freshly ground black pepper

3 cups tomato juice, well chilled

4 celery stalks, with leaves, to serve

serves 4

Half fill a large pitcher with crushed ice. Cut one of the lemons into slices and squeeze the juice from the others. Add to the pitcher, together with all the other ingredients except the celery. Mix well. Serve in highball glasses with a celery stalk.

virgin mary

1¼ cups tomato juice, well chilled

2 grinds of black pepper

½ teaspoon Tabasco sauce

2 dashes Worcestershire sauce

2 teaspoons fresh lemon juice

1 teaspoon horseradish sauce

2 celery stalks, with leaves, to serve

serves 2

Shake all the ingredients over ice and strain into a highball filled with ice. Garnish with a celery stalk.

index

conversion charts

Weights and measures have been
rounded up or down slightly to make
measuring easier.

Volume equivalents:

American	Metric	Imperial
1 teaspoon	5 ml	
1 tablespoon	15 ml	
¼ cup	60 ml	2 fl.oz.
⅓ cup	75 ml	2½ fl.oz.
½ cup	125 ml	4 fl.oz.
⅔ cup	150 ml	5 fl.oz. (¼ pint)
¾ cup	175 ml	6 fl.oz.
1 cup	250 ml	8 fl.oz.
1 stick butter = 8 tablespoons = 125 g		

Weight equivalents: **Measurements:**

Imperial	Metric	Inches	cm
1 oz.	25 g	¼ inch	5 mm
2 oz.	50 g	½ inch	1 cm
3 oz.	75 g	¾ inch	1.5 cm
4 oz.	125 g	1 inch	2.5 cm
5 oz.	150 g	2 inches	5 cm
6 oz.	175 g	3 inches	7 cm
7 oz.	200 g	4 inches	10 cm
8 oz. (½ lb.)	250 g	5 inches	12 cm
9 oz.	275 g	6 inches	15 cm
10 oz.	300 g	7 inches	18 cm
11 oz.	325 g	8 inches	20 cm
12 oz.	375 g	9 inches	23 cm
13 oz.	400 g	10 inches	25 cm
14 oz.	425 g	11 inches	28 cm
15 oz.	475 g	12 inches	30 cm
16 oz. (1 lb.)	500 g		
2 lb.	1 kg		

Oven temperatures:

110°C	(225°F)	Gas ¼
120°C	(250°F)	Gas ½
140°C	(275°F)	Gas 1
150°C	(300°F)	Gas 2
160°C	(325°F)	Gas 3
180°C	(350°F)	Gas 4
190°C	(375°F)	Gas 5
200°C	(400°F)	Gas 6
220°C	(425°F)	Gas 7
230°C	(450°F)	Gas 8
240°C	(475°F)	Gas 9

credits

Recipes

Louise Pickford
Fresh figs with ricotta & honeycomb
Panettone French toast with coconut milk
Sweet bruschetta with quince-glazed figs
Hash browns
Mushroom burgers
Homemade baked beans
Salmon & sweet potato fish cakes
Creamy eggs with goat cheese
Eggs Benedict
Kedgeree
Baby custard tarts
Soft-cooked eggs with asparagus soldiers
Pecan & chocolate muffins
Raspberry & rosewater lassi
Mango, coconut, & passion fruit shake
Campari fizz
Mimosa
Peach bellini
Walnut cake
Warm compote with peaches, apricots, & blueberries
Roasted mascarpone peaches
Baked eggs with smoked salmon & chives

Fran Warde
Winter dried fruit pot
Rhubarb & plum compote
Apple & pear compote
Plum & honey cup
Frozen berry yogurt cup
Banana & granola yogurt pot
Eggs cocotte
Raspberry, kiwi, & blueberry smoothie
Carrot, apple, & ginger smoothie
Fruit platter
House granola
Swiss muesli
Courgettes & cheddar on toast
Steak & tomato sandwich
Plum pastries
Kickstarter bloody Mary

Linda Collister
Muesli bars
Breakfast kabobs
Breakfast doughnuts
Granola round
Mini gingerbreads
Traditional pecan coffee cake
French toast
Marmalade muffins
Lemon, almond, & blueberry muffins
Fresh peach & oat muffins
Sticky buns
Banana pecan loaf
Breakfast tea loaf
Cinnamon raisin nut bread
Apple buttermilk scone round

Kate Habershon
Blueberry sour cream pancakes
Poppyseed pancakes
Triple chocolate pancakes
Date & pistachio griddle cakes
Apple whole-wheat waffles
Classic Belgian waffles
Morning-after breakfast waffles
Cornmeal & bacon breakfast stack
Raspberry waffles

Jennie Shapter
Classic Spanish tortilla
Sausage, potato, & onion tortilla
Smoked salmon omelet
Porcini frittata
Spinach & pancetta frittata
Baked brunch omelet
Feta cheese & tomato open omelet
Omelet wraps

Susanna Blake
Creamy orange French toast
Macerated berries on brioche French toast
Toasted brioche with lemon cream & fresh raspberries
Melting cheese & ham croissants
Toasted bagels with cream cheese & smoked salmon
Creamy scrambled eggs on rye
Eggs Florentine
Choc-mocha cupcakes

Rachael Anne Hill
Kickstart kabobs
Extra oaty porridge
All-in-one-oats
Bacon, tomato, & basil toasty
Herby cheese swirls
Sardine bruschetta

Maxine Clark
Tea-infused fruit compote
Sausage & bacon rolls
Uncooked freezer raspberry jam
Fluffy potato pancakes
Egg, mascarpone, & asparagus crostini

Lindy Wildsmith
Dried apricot conserve
Chunky lemon, lime, & grapefruit marmalade
Italian fig conserve
Red berry jelly
Rhubarb & ginger jam

Annie Nichols
Swiss rösti
Potato noodles
Golden potato biscuits

Clare Ferguson
Churros
Arepas with fruit batidas

Ben Reed
Virgin Mary

Celia Brooks Brown
Rarebit

Hattie Ellis
Text on coffee

Clare Gordon-Smith
Text on tea

Jane Noraika
Exotic fruit scrunch

Brian Glover
Lemon curd

Jennifer Joyce
Huevos rancheros

Elsa Petersen-Schepelern
Fruit & vegetables with yogurt dressing
Avocado salad
Rosemary tisane
Blueberry & orange smoothie
Berry, apricot, & orange slush
Red berry smoothie
Banana & papaya smoothie
Iced lime tea
Hot lemon tea
Mint tea
Minty ginger Granny Smith
Pineapple crush
Watermelon & lime slush

Photography

Key: a=above, b=below, r=right, l=left, c=center.

William Lingwood
Page 1, 3cl, 27, 36c, 37, 39, 40, 43, 44, 47, 48, 51, 60, 64, 68, 71, 73, 77, 85, 86, 97, 112l, 115, 120, 204l, 204r, 205, 211, 212, 215, 216, 219, 220, 224, 227, 231, 232, 240

Ian Wallace
Pages 6br, 7, 9, 12, 15, 28, 63, 67, 74, 81, 93, 105, 112r, 116, 119, 127, 131, 150c, 150r, 153, 161, 173, 223

Tara Fisher
Pages 112c, 113, 135, 136, 139, 140, 143, 144, 147, 148, 188c, 189, 192, 196, 199, 200, 203

Debi Treloar
Pages 2, 3cr, 6ac, 6acc, 6bcc, 8l, 16, 31, 70l, 70r, 101, 106, 165, 207, 208, 235

Philip Webb
Pages 3r, 59, 98, 150l, 151, 154, 157, 158, 162, 174, 177, 178, 182

David Brittain
Pages 4, 6al, 6cl, 6bl, 6ar, 6acr, 6bcr

Noel Murphy
Pages 5, 23, 82, 102, 195, endpapers

Peter Cassidy
Pages 20, 55, 109, 110, 123

Caroline Arber
Page 11, 19, 124, 228

Nicky Dowey
Pages 24, 32, 90, 186

Francesca Yorke
Pages 8c, 8r, 36l, 188r

Martin Brigdale
Pages 52, 132, 166

Peter Myers
Pages 89, 94, 185

Polly Wreford
Pages 6bc, 35, 78

Jean Cazals
Pages 70c, 204c

Diana Miller
Pages 169, 170

Gus Filgate
Page 128

Jeremy Hopley
Page 56

Richard Jung
Page 191

Sandra Lane
Page 188l

David Munns
Page 3l

Pia Tryde
Page 36r

Patrice de Villiers
Page 181